CALL OF THE MOUNTAINS

With deep gratitude to this book's sponsors:

INLAND VALLEY
Daily Bulletin

THE SUN

CALL OF THE MOUNTAINS

The Beauty and Legacy of Southern California's San Jacinto,
San Bernardino, and San Gabriel Mountains

Ann and Farley Olander

Stephens Press • Las Vegas, Nevada

Photography: Farley Olander
Editor: Laura Brundige
Design: Chris Wheeler
Layout: Sue Campbell

ISBN 1-932173-46-3

CIP Data Available

Stephens
Press LLC

A Stephens Media Group Company
Post Office Box 1600
Las Vegas, NV 89125-1600
www.stephenspress.com

Printed in Hong Kong

To the mountains' guardians past and present.

CALL OF THE
CON

The Beauty and

MOUNTAINS
TENTS

Legacy of Southern California's San Jacinto, San Bernardino, and San Gabriel Mountains

Above: This hydraulic operation was short-lived. To get enough water, the Hocamac Mining Company built a two-mile pipeline from San Antonio Creek's headwaters. But the system's waste water polluted the creek downstream, which forced limited operations and made their mining ventures ultimately unprofitable. Circa. 1894, Henry E. Huntington Library, courtesy of John W. Robinson.

Below: Noted historian and author John Robinson leads a Sierra Club group to the former hydraulic mining site on Baldy Notch. He identifies the location by a tree located on the right side of both pictures.

Foreword

Mountains sprawl over a generous portion of Southern California's landscape. They form an imposing bulwark separating the coastal plains and valleys from the interior arid lands, protecting the seaward lowlands from the desert's harshness. They gather precious moisture from Pacific storms, nourishing the lands below.

But more than these physical attributes, our mountains have an intrinsic value to humankind as sanctuaries where people can redeem and revitalize themselves away from the pressures of urban life. John Muir said it best: Mountains are "temples for mankind," where one can go to receive inspiration and renewal amid nature's handiwork.

In Southern California, three mountain ranges predominate, their highest summits reaching elevations in excess of 10,000 feet — the San Gabriels, the San Bernardinos, the San Jacintos.

Extending across the northern skyline of the Los Angeles Basin, the San Gabriel and Pomona valleys are the San Gabriel Mountains. Whether phantomlike behind a veil of grayish haze, sharply etched against a blue winter sky, or playing

hide-and-seek with billowing clouds, they are a familiar scene to the millions living below.

From a distance the San Gabriels sometimes appear austere and uninviting. But enter one of the many canyons that crease the face of the mountains and a whole new world appears. You stroll alongside a sparkling stream, its musical waters revealing a delightful diversity of moods — now dancing merrily over the pebble-strewn floor, then pausing in limpid pool, only to plunge over a miniature waterfall to begin a new life cycle. Overhead is a verdant canopy of live oak, sycamore, alder and bay.

The hillsides above are clothed in chaparral, that elfin forest of stiff, thorny shrubs and dwarf trees. Chaparral, which blankets about 75% of the Southern California mountains, has been damned as "too low to give shade, too high to see over, and too thick to go through." Anyone so foolish as to venture off road or trail and crawl through this brushy maze will soon come to believe there is a personal hostility in the unyielding branches and scratchy leaves.

A different experience awaits those who consider this elfin forest as a friend to visit, not as an enemy to thrash through. In bloom, much of the chaparral is sprinkled with colorful flowers. And what is more pleasing to the nature lover than ceonothus blooming a misty blue or white, California laurel unfolding masses of yellow flowers, or wild lilac giving forth its sweet aroma after a spring rain?

Above the chaparral, and sometimes enclaves within it, is the stately domain of conifers: first

Chaparral . . . has been damned as "too low to give shade, too high to see over, and too thick to go through."

big cone Douglas fir, then progressively higher, Jeffrey pine, Coulter pine, incense cedar, sugar pine, white fir, lodgepole pine. On the highest ridges sub alpine conditions reign, and a scattering of gnarled limber pines live a marginal existence among windswept crags. Lording over all the San Gabriels is the bald, roundish summit of Mount San Antonio, better known to most as Mount Baldy.

Cajon Pass and the slanted troughs of the mighty San Andreas Fault separate the San Gabriels from the San Bernardinos. The latter rise, rather abruptly at first, in chaparral-coated slopes to the 5,000-foot summits of Cleghorn and Cajon mountains. Eastward from here, for some thirty miles, the crest of the San Bernardinos is remarkably uniform. Undulating ridges and tapered hillsides conceal within their folds verdant glens and sparkling blue lakes. This crest country, much of it covered with forest as magnificent as any in Southern California (alas, until the ravages of the bark beetle), is the home to thousands of residents and vacationers. The communities of Crestline, Lake Gregory, Blue Jay, Lake Arrowhead, Running Springs and Big Bear make up the urbanized San Bernardinos.

From Big Bear Lake, the San Bernardinos veer southward and, beyond the deep valley of the upper San Ana River, reach their majestic heights in the San Gorgonio Wilderness. Here the hiker and lover of pristine mountain country can rejoice. Lodgepole pine is the dominant conifer, standing tall of the sheltered slopes, twisted low on the windswept timberline ridges. Tumbling creeks flow icy cold. Hidden within the high mountain folds are the gems of Dollar and Dry lakes. Reigning over all is 11,499-foot San Gorgonio Mountain, also known as Grayback, the rooftop of Southern California. The great hogback mountain is the culminating hump of the 10,000-foot, seven-mile long, sky-piercing ridge that dominates the wilderness. Here snow patches linger well into early summer. The air is crisp with the chill of elevation. The sky is deep blue, free of the urban-generated murkiness that so often clogs the lower elevations.

The broad gap of San Gorgonio Pass separates the San Bernardinos from Southern California's third great mountain range, the San Jacintos. The San Jacintos, granitic in structure, more resemble the Sierra Nevada than any other Southern California range. Most impressive and Sierra-like is the stupendous northeast face of 10,804-foot San Jacinto Peak, soaring almost 10,000 vertical feet in less than five horizontal miles. Somber gray in summer and fall, gleaming white in winter, snow-streaked by late spring, San Jacinto's vaulting desert face has fired the imagination and artistry of many a painter and photographer and awed countless Palm Springs visitors.

San Jacinto, as is true with most mountains, has its gentle as well as its rugged features. The southwest flank of the mountain mass is made up of rolling hills and ridges that rise from the San Jacinto Valley and become progressively higher and steeper until they culminate at the summit. Nestled in Strawberry Valley, close under the granite crags of Lily Rock and Tahquitz

San Jacinto's vaulting desert face has fired the imagination and artistry of many a painter and photographer and awed countless Palm Springs visitors.

Peak, is the charming little mountain community in Idyllwild.

But it is the summit country of the San Jacintos that is most alluring. Here, well above the highways and byways that wind around the lower and middle slopes, is a sky island of detectable alpine wilderness, unsurpassed in Southern California. Tahquitz Meadow, Long Valley, Round Valley, Little Round Valley are grassy oases, nourished by springs and threaded by sparkling creeks that tumble and cascade down the mountain. In season, alpine wildflowers add a beautiful dash of color. This mountain roof garden is a hiker's paradise. Fortunately, most of it is preserved from civilization's encroachment by Mount San Jacinto Wilderness State Park and the federal San Jacinto Wilderness.

To really know our Southern California Mountains, you must leave the road and venture forth on foot. Only then can you fully experience the richness and sublimity of unspoiled nature. Over half a century I have walked the forest trails, forded the creeks, scrambled up the peaks for far-reaching vistas. It has been a soul nourishing experience.

Farley and Ann Olander, in beautiful photographs and eloquent, graceful prose, have crafted a moving tribute to our splendid mountains. Their work epitomizes our need to protect and preserve the diminishing wild areas of the San Gabriels, San Bernardinos, and San Jacintos from encroaching civilization.

— JOHN W. ROBINSON

Acknowledgements

Many people had an impact in shaping this book. I am grateful to each one and can only name a few here — family and friends, editors and publisher, as well as individuals who shared their mountain stories and provided needed information.

Phil Poretta, former president of the Billy Holcomb Chapter of E. Clampus Vitus, shared his research and knowledge of mining history in Holcomb Valley. This tireless source of information, Farley's longtime friend and running partner, led us to many sites and related details along the way.

I am indebted to the personnel at the Malki Musuem on the Morongo Indian Reservation. They steered me to books and an event with Katherine Siva Saubel, Cahuilla Indian elder, helping me to better understand Cahuilla influence in the San Jacinto Mountains.

On the Idyllwild Arts campus, Headmaster Bill Lohman and Director of Public Relations Darren Schilling enabled close-up visits and provided help whenever I asked. Head Librarian Jane Craford, who consistently found needed resources, connected me with Bob Krone, son of campus founders, Max and Bee Krone.

In addition I thank Michael P. Hamilton, Director of the UC James San Jacinto Mountains Reserve, for allowing us to visit the site when he was out of the country, and for Kevin Browne, information manager, who showed us their robotic cameras and research facilities — where Harry and Grace James once operated their Trailfinder School for Boys, inspiration for Pat Chapman, another individual to whom I'm indebted. She made time to reminisce about the Chapman Ranch School's experiential mountain learning situations near Mount Baldy. Similarly, thanks go to Kathy Farley, director and CEO of Arrowhead Ranch Outdoor Science School. She told us candid stories of the school's nearly 50-year history as she guided us about the new campus flush with sixth-graders in residence for the week.

One friend's contact often led to others. Particularly, I thank Ann Robinson, who introduced me to her colleagues in the San Gorgonio Wilderness Association. On various occasions, these committed volunteers spent time talking over the challenges and rewards of their work, which gave me new understanding about our precarious wilderness. I particularly thank volunteer coordinator John Flippin — who arranged for Farley and me to accompany volunteers Larry Stiles and Walter Roth on an overnight assignment — and equestrian coordinator Valerie Silva, who made it possible for us to accompany her on duty.

I appreciate interviewing many volunteers associated with other entities such as the Scenic Mount Lowe Railway Historical Committee; Angeles Volunteer Association Inc.; Forest Service Volunteer Association, San Jacinto Ranger District; and San Bernardino National Forest Volunteer Association coordinating the Big Bear Discovery Center, National Children's Forest and Fire Lookout Hosts. Special thanks go to Kirk Cloyd, president of the Riverside Mountain Rescue Unit, Inc., and Bill Reeves, executive director of the Fisheries Resource Volunteer Corps, who took extra time to explain the commitment behind their work.

Surveyor Mike Duffy answered my endless naïve questions as we accompanied his entourage up San Bernardino Peak for the Sesquicentennial Anniversary Celebration of the initial point monument there. I am grateful for his patient answers about surveying as well as stories about the monument's history. I thank Chuck Medrud, who first introduced me to the Cucamonga Creek Canyon and who inspired the community cleanup. I also appreciate Brian Elliott, one of the volunteers on that project, who shared some poignant memories of completing the grueling Angeles Crest 100-mile mountain race.

Writing this book would have been difficult without valued consideration from the national forests and state park personnel, who repeatedly took time out to explain issues and tell about their enthusiasm for our mountains. In the San Bernardino National Forest I am particularly indebted to Gabe Garcia, front country district ranger and Ron Huxman, special agent, and in Mount San Jacinto State Park, Jerald A. Frates, supervising state park ranger. In the Angeles National Forest, San Gabriel River Ranger District, I thank especially Barbara Croonquist, interpretive specialist; Steve Segretto, naturalist; Rick Dean, educator; and Lois Pickens, volunteer coordinator.

Sierra Club friends and leaders — including Ralph Salisbury, John Monson, Tim Allyn, Joyce Burk, Judy Smith, Joe Whyte, Peter Jorris, George Wysup, Will Vanderwilt, Doug Thomson, Janice and Brian Elliott, David and Patty Thorne — have provided invaluable opportunities to explore new areas and discuss ways to enjoy yet protect our mountains, the impetus behind this photo-essay. Heartfelt thanks goes especially to John Robinson. While writing *Call of the Mountains*, I turned to Robinson's books as the best documented resource on the area's mountain and mining history. His influence, however, goes further. Throughout the years, we have routinely checked Robinson's hiking guides before hitting the trails. In fact we've worn out more than one edition of his legendary books, which vibrate with his knowledge, research and love of these mountains.

For encouragement and support, I'd like to thank Barbara Frey, Judy Wolfe, Diana Brown, Debbie Council, Dot and Al Rhodes, Judy and George Abell, Janet and Ken Kaufman and our adult children, Andy, Katie and especially Doug, who read sections of my earlier drafts. I appreciate my parents, Kathleen and Imon Bartley who taught me to believe in realizing dreams. Although my deceased father never lived close to mountains, he loved traveling to them and influenced my exhilaration in them. Above all, I thank my husband Farley, partner in this photo-essay. *Call of the Mountains* results from his images along with his patience to read and discuss innumerable preliminary drafts.

I would like to thank Frances Young, my former city news editor at the *Inland Valley Daily Bulletin*, who taught me newspaper skills invaluable in writing this photo-essay. For helping identify plants, I appreciate Rancho Santa Ana Botanic Garden herbarium curator Steve Boyd and former curator and taxnomist Robert Folger Thorne, professor emeritus, Claremont Graduate University. Thanks also go to Laura Brundige for her unflagging editorial help, creative designer Chris Wheeler, who brought the book's concept alive, and to book designer extraordinaire Sue Campbell. Tasha Cortez, project manager and Dan Love, graphic designer, both of whom kept all the pieces in order. Finally, I thank Jim Burns, president of the Hayes Group, LLC, who believed in *Call of the Mountains* from the beginning, publisher Carolyn Hayes Uber, president of Stephens Press, who made it happen and to the *Inland Valley Daily Bulletin* and the *San Bernardino Sun* for their generous sponsorship of this book.

— ANN OLANDER

Climb the mountains and get their good tidings. Nature's peace will flow into you as sunshine flows into trees. The winds will blow their own freshness into you, and the storms their energy, while cares will drop off like autumn leaves.

— JOHN MUIR

Our Mountains

When I first moved to Southern California some thirty-six years ago it was easy to get lost driving among housing tracts and vineyards. I soon learned, however, that if the weather was clear I needed only to take a bearing on the mountains and they would guide me home. That was my first awareness of the three ranges that surround us.

An 8,500-foot ridgeline rises 7,000 feet just outside my front door. Even when obscured by fog — or smog — this mighty span lifts my spirits. It steadfastly reminds me that the mountains endure, patiently beckoning us to their sanctuaries.

On clear days Southern California's highest peaks are visible in the San Jacinto, San Bernardino and San Gabriel Mountains. Urban sprawl, however, has begun to threaten their beauty, habitat and watershed. Los Angeles County is growing every 10 years by more than a half-million people, and growth rates are escalating

These are my mountains — Ontario and Cucamonga Peaks in the San Garbriels, as we see them through the blossoming nectarine tree in our front yard.

in adjacent Riverside and San Bernardino Counties as well. Most of these counties' residents live within an hour's drive of pristine, wild places, many that are vulnerable to unchecked development. So, with my husband, Farley, as chief photographer and colleague, I set out 18 months ago to remind us of their wonder, champion their beauty and inspire their preservation.

From years of outings, predominately hiking, I thought I knew the three ranges. But our many mountain weekends took us to new areas and surprised us with fresh understanding of even the most familiar haunts.

Compelling moments kept our commitment fueled. Two large deer bounded gracefully from Round Valley's underbrush, so close that we almost touched. A young woman exulted in a mountain "high" as she summated 10,834-foot San Jacinto Peak for the first time. A flaming red sunset viewed from San Gorgonio Pass bonded us spiritually with an older man who lived nearby and stepped outside to marvel at its glory with us. "I've been watching sunsets here for 46 years, and I never get tired of it. It's always wonderful," he smiled, naming the peaks as they receded, one by one, into the afterglow. The open field that provided our vantage point, he added proudly, would soon become a public park, keeping these sunset vistas possible in the future.

Weekend after weekend I met people basking in similar moments — and people responding to the mountains' call.

I believe that our responses are crucial for future generations, that they too can know the mountains' wonder and beauty.

Above: South Fork Meadow invites us to sit beside its singing springs among green grasses dotted with yellow wildflowers. This verdant oasis in the San Gorgonio Wilderness is closed for overnight camping — to allow for meadow restoration. Yet spending even a few minutes here can help restore a weary soul.

Right: We look to the mountains to guide us home. In this case, 8,859-foot Cucamonga Peak appears directly over Hermosa Avenue in Rancho Cucamonga.

Below: On a clear day from Kenneth Hahn State Recreation Area in Los Angeles, the San Gabriel Mountains loom above the city skyscrapers. Mount San Antonio, better known as Old Baldy or Mount Baldy, dominates at 10,064 feet.

Mountain peaks light up to a
flaming red. Then while we watch
from our upstairs window,
they recede one by one
in the setting sun.

The wilderness that has come to us from the eternity of the past
we have the boldness to project into the eternity of the future.

— HOWARD ZAHNISER

Legacy

Lamps swayed and windows rattled as though a giant were shaking our house like a toy. It was the 1971 Sylmar earthquake. Relatives back East continued to envy our life in sunny, warm Southern California in spite of that earthquake following two years of record floods, fires, and Santa Ana winds that approached 100 miles per hour. Neither these Eastern admirers nor we ourselves understand, perhaps, how directly our lives are influenced by the San Jacinto, San Bernardino and San Gabriel Mountains. Earthquakes shape the mountains, which in turn shape our famous mild weather and influence our infamous fires, floods and high winds. But human stories, gentle and adventurous, shape the mountain legacy that we enjoy.

All three ranges shelter bedrock mortars where Native Americans ground acorns, seeds and other nuts, as in Palm Canyon on the desert side of the San Jacintos. Visiting the scene where wom-

Old Baldy glistens in the west as hikers make their way down to the Icehouse Saddle from Timber Mountain.

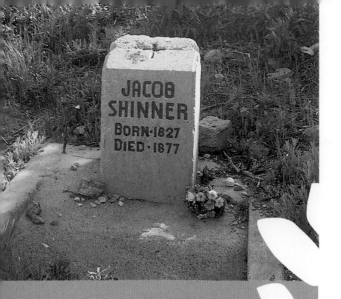

The ghost of Jacob Shiner the one-legged miner

roams the Baldy area, appearing from time to time in the village. Apparently, people have reported seeing his ghost in several different places, and at least one young woman remembers how the stories — or even the rhyme — frightened her at night when she was small.

Another source told me that Shiner worked mines in several places, from the Iron Fork area all the way across Cattle Canyon into upper San Antonio Canyon. Reportedly, he died after losing his leg in a mining accident.

Originally Shiner was buried on the east side of the road entering Mt. Baldy village, so one source said. When building the new road, the crew moved his body to the west side and placed an unmarked pile of graves on the new site. Is that why his ghost roamed, I wondered? But the pile of rocks — witnessed by several locals — is no longer there today.

Instead, Jacob Shiner has a real tombstone. His last name has been spelled there as Shinner, which doesn't rhyme with miner. Perhaps because of the non-rhyming spelling, or thanks to the fresh flowers placed beside the tombstone as on April, 2004, Jacob's ghost no longer needs to roam.

en long ago prepared the family's food creates a momentary link through time and space. Several of our friends like to relive the gold rush days and explore old mill sites. These reminders of a feverish era are slowly disintegrating near remote streambeds or on isolated mountain slopes. Yet the miners' tales live on.

When we first moved here, my uncle liked to point out the convoluted jumble along the San Andreas Fault at Cajon Pass, where the San Gabriel Mountains almost abut with the San Bernardino Range. San Gorgonio Pass separates this range from the San Jacintos, which seemed more familiar to me at the time, because in places they reminded me of the Rocky Mountains and the Sierra Nevada.

Sometimes the peaks in our local mountains are referred to as "islands in the sky," towering above urban centers and desert. They fit that appellation perfectly when you're above the clouds and the peaks seem to float, disconnected, above the hustle of everyday life.

And, each range has its highest, signature peak. Mount San Jacinto seems to sweep its entire vertical 10,834-feet from the desert floor near Palm Springs. From the summit on one memorable

Top: Formed by movement along the San Andreas Fault, Cajon Pass separates the San Gabriel Mountains from the San Bernardinos. Trains like this one thread their way through the jumbled cleft where pioneers once entered Southern California.

Below: Mount San Jacinto seems to vault up its entire 10,834 feet from this rest stop on the I-10 Freeway, similar to how it appears to sweep its full vertical distance from the desert floor near Palm Springs.

Native Americans ground acorns, seeds and nuts into meal in bedrock mortar holes, like this one in Palm Canyon, San Jacintos. Similar food-processing cultural sites can be found in all three mountain ranges shown in this book.

Mount San Antonio (Mount Baldy or Old Baldy) and other
San Gabriel peaks float above the clouds in the distant right,
looking west from the San Bernardino Peak Trail

occasion, we watched clouds drift about like enormous puffs of cotton candy.

Mount San Gorgonio, nicknamed "Old Greyback," dominates over ten other peaks that rise above 10,000 feet in the San Bernardinos. Anyone traversing the long, bare approach to its 11,499-foot summit appreciates that "San G," as local teenagers have dubbed it, is Southern California's highest mountain.

Mount San Antonio rules the San Gabriels. Its broad and bare 10,064-foot summit makes it easily identifiable throughout the greater Los Angeles area and begs its nickname, "Old Baldy." West of the Baldy area, ridges follow in waves. Chaparral-covered slopes and boulder-strewn washes lead to rugged canyons and a surprising number of waterfalls.

Getting to these peaks is easier today than it was for my generation's grandparents, even though fires and floods have destroyed countless trails and structures. The 1938 flood, for example, wiped out popular resorts such as Camp Baldy in San Antonio Canyon, which provided a temporary base for tourist parties in elaborate hiking costumes. Now, we zoom up the Angeles Crest and Rim-of-the-World Highways, getting to the high country readily; yet ironically, this accessibility adds to the challenge of preserving the sites we come to explore.

Mountain communities have mushroomed, providing homes for permanent and weekend residents. I have favorite getaways in all three ranges, where I treasure memories of weekend church retreats and camps for our children. Public and private campgrounds abound. School classrooms come to the mountains as do multi-aged groups representing diverse interests. My bird watching friends delight in Eaton Canyon, while angler friends like casting in

Top: It is not the top of the world, but the top of Southern California where 11,499-foot San Gorgonio Mountain climaxes the ridgeline seen from near the San Bernardino Peak Divide Trail.

Above: Rose-colored prickly phlox, Leptodactylon californicum, warms the heart on a foggy spring day above Switzer Falls in the San Gabriel Mountains.

Below: This paved road, closed to motorized vehicles along the West Fork of the San Gabriel River, makes an ideal training location for club members of the Southern California Road Runners.

Sturtevant Fall's plunging sprays greet all who stroll here from Chantry Flat in the San Gabriel Mountains.

Bear Creek. The list seems infinite — wildflower aficionados, equestrians, families, and individuals.

Clubs flourish for walkers, runners, hikers and cyclists. We who live in the area have an advantage, if training to hike up Half Dome, Mount Whitney or more ambitious summits. Runners compete yearly in the Baldy Peaks 50K, Angeles Crest 100, and other runs-to-the-top of various peaks. All types of athletes come to train here, using the altitude to build lung capacity and stamina.

The ongoing challenge, however, is keeping our mountains available for enjoyment while safeguarding their allure. Our stewardship legacy traces back to the earliest Native American inhabitants. In the 1880s, when excessive timber cutting threatened to devastate local mountains, valley residents worked with John Muir and others across the country to protect our nation's forests. The resultant Forest Reserve Act of 1891 paved the way for establishing timberland reserves, re-

"The wilderness that has come to us from the eternity of the past we have the boldness to project into the eternity of the future,"
HOWARD ZAHNISER

named soon after as national forests. The Angeles and San Bernardino National Forests encompass the three mountain ranges featured in this book.

In the 1900s, area residents like Harry James worked tirelessly to secure federal preservation of our primitive, wild areas. The Wilderness Act of 1964 designated 9,140,000 acres as protected wilderness — wilderness that protects pristine landscape, wildlife, and watershed — wilderness that gives us places for spiritual renewal and sustainable recreation.

"The wilderness that has come to us from the eternity of the past we have the boldness to project into the eternity of the future," wrote the bill's author Howard Zahniser, cousin of an Inland Valley friend of ours. Locally the bill established the San Gabriel, Cucamonga, Mount San Jacinto and San Gorgonio Wilderness Areas and led to additional protection in these mountains with the California Wilderness Act of 1984.

Mountain popularity, however, proliferates as the area's population expands. Around 3.5 mil-

These twisted branches frame Mount San Jacinto beyond massive Yucaipa Ridge. This early spring scene stopped hikers approaching the San Bernardino Peak Divide Trail from Mill Creek.

Hikers zigzag down switchbacks on the San Bernardino Peak Trail

San Gorgonio Wilderness Association volunteer Bob Williams filters drinking water from High Creek on the Vivian Creek Trail.

lion people a year visit the Angeles National Forest. About 100,000 visitors enter the San Gorgonio Wilderness yearly, even with a permit system in effect. Hence efforts continue to preserve our forests and remaining roadless areas. At the time of this writing, July 2004, the public is giving input to the Forest Service's master plan revisions, as required by law every 10 to 15 years. In addition, two California bills are before Congress that would include wilderness designation for several local qualifying roadless areas.

Meanwhile, motivated by budget cuts and a heightened sense of maintaining our mountains, volunteers are stepping in. Everywhere I went during these 18 months I discovered people working in sundry ways, like Bob Williams, San Gorgonio Wilderness Association volunteer. On his days off, Williams helps maintain trails and checks backcountry permits. "It's a great opportunity to give back," he said, pausing as he picked up trash near the Vivian Creek Trail.

Volunteers monitor stream resources, maintain trails, provide visitor information, restore

Boulders along the North Fork of the San Jacinto River form the outline of a face, while butterflies flitter about the scarlet monkey flowers, Mimulus cardinalis.

. . . wild places give smog-bleary, clatter-weary city dwellers opportunities to find clean air and solitude . . .

historic sites, and remove graffiti. They help with children's programs, watershed restoration, plant and wildlife surveys, fire-lookout duty, wilderness interpretation, and rescue patrol. One experienced hiker friend appreciates the latter service most especially, as it saved his life. Rugged wild areas, often minutes from urban lights, can be deceiving. Friable granite rocks can make the steep slopes slippery, even without icy conditions. Radical weather changes can prompt accidents, and a few steps off trail can disorient even veteran hikers.

Nonetheless we keep returning to our mountains. Their wild places give smog-bleary, clatter-weary city dwellers opportunities to find clean air and solitude, to see bighorn sheep at sunset, and to encounter more trees than people. Each mountain range spins 1,001 tales, sagas of adventure, discovery and dreams.

31

We simply need that wild country available to us, even if we never do more than drive to its edge and look in. For it can be a means of reassuring ourselves of our sanity as creatures, a part of the geography of hope.

— WALLACE STEGNER, FROM *The Sound of Mountain Water.*

Album I

Mountain Moments

Come listen to an enchanting anthem of trickling spring water in South Fork Meadow's cathedral of green, decorated with the soft floral yellows. San Gorgonio Wilderness, San Bernardino Mountains.

Left: White-barked aspen trees reach for the heavens, while their golden leaves shimmer against the blue October sky. Aspen Grove near Hart Bar Campground, San Bernardino Mountains.

Right: What can be lovelier than the graceful California bluebell, also called wild Canterbury bell, Phacelia minor? These prolific bells herald springtime throughout the foothills. Chantry Flat, San Gabriel Mountains.

Bottom: Solitude on top of Mount Baldy gives time for pondering, and the distant islands-in-the-sky help orient the spirit, transcending immediate concerns. Authors' son Andrew, San Gabriel Mountains.

Previous page: Reflections on Jackson Lake go deeper than the water's surface. A popular place for family picnics and walking dogs, this lake is a sag pond created by the San Andreas Fault. Near Wrightwood, San Gabriel Mountains.

Above: The white Prickly Poppy, Argemone mumita, stands out in the open, offering a friendly surprise in spite of its prickles. Lower reach of Vivian Creek Trail, San Gorgonio Wilderness.

Right: A hiker winds her way up the Fuller Ridge Trail around granite outcroppings, with the San Gorgonio Massif looming in the distance. One of the least traveled routes up San Jacinto Peak, the trail passes several springs along the way.

One more step, then another. It's hard work, plodding through snow in cold, thin air up 10,691-foot San Bernardino East Peak. But the exhilaration upon reaching the summit under this deep, blue sky makes it all worthwhile. San Gorgonio Wilderness.

Take care of the land, and it will take care of you.
— KATHERINE SIVA SAUBEL

Mountain Mystique

The Cahuilla elder sat so unobtrusively, just inside the door of Morongo Indian Reservation's tiny Malki Museum, that I did not notice her at first. Then she began to speak: "We were put here to be caretakers of the earth, not destroyers. And we are still here."

Katherine Siva Saubel's melodious voice spilled over the intricate Cahuilla baskets, dusty ceremonial artifacts, and about 30 of us who had crowded into the room's narrow aisle. Saubel, a descendent of the San Jacintos' earliest inhabitants, and anthropologist Lowell John Bean had agreed to share Cahuilla wisdom that day as part of a work party at the museum Saubel had co-founded in 1964. So, under the inscrutable gaze of Mount San Jacinto across Interstate 10, we had planted agaves and sages in the museum's ethno-botanical garden all morning, anticipating the privilege of listening to their teaching.

San Jacinto Peak glows with tints of red in the fading sun, as seen from San Gongonio Pass on I-10 Freeway. The authors found a quick exit in Beaumont to bask in this ephemeral scene.

A hiker stops to catch her breath and marvel at the shoulder-high lupine, *Lupinus polyphyllus,* as she nears Wellman Cienega on the trail to San Jacinto Peak.

From the summit of Cahuilla Mountain, tree branches form an arch revealing San Jacinto Peak, sacred to the Cahuilla peoples.

Spring winds howled through San Gorgonio Pass, and 84-year-old Saubel remained bundled up with a bright orange and turquoise scarf pulled snugly over her head. Like other elders, Saubel had seen countless changes — changes compelling her to preserve Cahuilla knowledge, to keep journaling, lecturing at universities, and writing books on Cahuilla language, culture and ethno-botany. She attributed her ultimate advice to the Creator: *"Take care of the land, and it will take care of you."*

Human habitation in the San Jacintos began with the Cahuilla; traces of Native American mystique exist still throughout the range — on trails winding through hip-high lupine under craggy peaks, near a campus meadow where music soars, and at a nature reserve set aside for study.

The Agua Caliente tribe of Cahuillas in the Palm Springs area maintains visitor access to several San Jacinto canyons where their ancestors once lived. Red-tailed hawks swoop after ravens in the cliffs above seasonal waterfalls and famed palm oases. During a March visit to Palm Canyon, a tribal ranger explained snake habitat to a group

I only went out for a walk and finally concluded to stay out 'til sundown, for going out, I found was really going in.
— John Muir

of youngsters gathered under a palm tree while an elderly couple set up a picnic nearby.

Cahuillas also thrived on the San Jacintos' western slopes, the setting of Helen Hunt's 1884 romantic novel *Ramona*, which is re-enacted annually in the Ramona Bowl near Hemet. The fictionalized story, based on a Cahuilla couple's intolerance-based tragedy, brought awareness of the Cahuillas' plight — and more pioneers — to the alluring San Jacintos at the turn of the century.

The real Ramona and her husband lived on a flat of Cahuilla Mountain where, one day last spring, only a few motorcycles broke the silence. Walking to the summit away from the dirt road, I heard only my feet crunching the earth and the occasional whirr of hummingbirds. I pictured Ramona gathering acorns in the nearby oak grove and grinding them in bedrock mortar holes. Perhaps she didn't walk on to the summit, but my climb rewarded me with splendid views of San Jacinto Peak, sacred to Cahuilla peoples.

One hardly thinks of palm trees in the mountains, yet several canyons along the eastern flanks of the San Jacintos support oases like this one in Palm Canyon near Palm Springs. These stately California fan palms, *Washingtonia filifera*, are reportedly the largest such stand in the world.

Top: *Lisa Steckley basks in the vista from the summit of San Jacinto Peak. Across San Gorgonio Pass, clouds are gathering over San Gorgonio Mountain, Southern California's highest. But it doesn't diminish the moment.*

Above: *Lupine and manzanita line this portion of the trail, above lush Wellman Cienega, on the popular eight-mile route to San Jacinto Peak from Humber Park.*

San Jacinto's mystique beguiles its visitors and lures us in, whether we view it from afar or follow its trails. Four other mountains in the range tower above 10,000 feet, but Mount San Jacinto dominates over all. As is the case with most mountains, reaching the summit brings a singular "aha." Yet the hushed aura surrounding San Jacinto's boulder-jumbled peak always surprises me, regardless of the season or choice of trail to get there. Hikers wait quietly for friends to photograph them beside the 10, 834-foot elevation marker while others crouch beside the boulders for wind shelter or look at the encircling views, which on a clear day include the ocean, desert, mountains, and valley.

Several trails to the peak wind upward through different life zones, but I like best the fern-adorned meadows, seeping springs, and seasonal wildflowers. The popular eight-mile route from Humber Park winds through such an oasis, Wellman Cienega. One of the least traveled routes is the Fuller Ridge Trail, beginning northwest of Idyllwild, while the shortest and most heavily traveled route leads five and a half miles from the Palm Springs Aerial Tram.

Eighty some passengers sigh a collective "whoooo" each time the revolving tramcar passes a support tower, swaying and dipping as if released momentarily into mid-air. The Palm Spring Aerial Tram, first opened in 1963, whisks visitors from palms to pines, up almost 6,000 vertical feet to Long Valley and the Mount San Jacinto State Park Wilderness.

Above: Splashes of red Indian paintbrush, a Castilleja *species, contrast with the lush green of ferns in Wellman Cienega.*

Right: Lodgepole pines encircle Round Valley, a lush meadow two miles from Long Valley. Carpeted with grasses and wildflowers in the summer or coated with snow in the winter, this area is a popular year-round destination for backpackers and hikers of all ages.

Below: During mid-summer this showy lupine Lupinus polyphyllus *blooms en masse along a portion of the Wellman Cienega Route.*

"The tram's a real benefit for people who wouldn't be able to come up here otherwise," comments Jerald Frates, supervising state park ranger. Increased numbers of visitors, however, threaten the pristine character of the wilderness, and environmentalists voice concern. In 1971, the state and U.S. Forest Service developed wilderness permit systems, establishing various quotas.

In the summer of 2003, with a full parking lot below, we encountered surprisingly few people away from the tram terminus and fewer yet beyond the Long Valley Ranger Station in designated wilderness. The two-mile trail winding up to Round Valley seemed no busier than in the early 1980s when we'd backpacked there with our young children, which was possible thanks to the tram.

Two days after Christmas, 2003, we rode the tram again, for an easy snow hike to Round Valley with one of our sons. Away from the station terminus where bundled-up frolickers coasted on sleds, we stepped into a silent, glittering world. Five to six inches of new powdery snow had fallen, and as long as I didn't stop to admire the snow-covered trees I kept warm in spite of the temperature's hovering near 20 degrees Fahrenheit. Round Valley sparkled in the mid-morning sunshine and I felt exhilarated, surrounded by snowy ridges and icicle-bedecked pines.

Just before we turned back toward the tram, our son spotted fresh footprints leading in the direction of San Jacinto Peak. Seasoned hikers, we were prepared with water, food, extra clothes, and hiking poles, so the three of us established a turn-around time — to be adjusted sooner if the trail became icy — and followed the footprints through a shimmering fairyland. They led us to Wellman Divide, which was framed by glittering, snow-laden trees sparkling against a clear blue sky. Beyond the Divide slopes of manzanita and chinquapin were clothed in knuckles of ice. We arrived at an arctic-appearing peak — its boulders molded together in crystalline, gargantuan shapes — at turn-around time, just after meeting the trailblazers whose footprints we'd followed.

Such magical moments for visitors extend throughout the range, and volunteers help keep those moments possible. Kirk Cloyd, president of

Above: The Palm Springs Aerial Tram whisks passengers from palms to pines, about 6,000 vertical feet from the desert to Long Valley and the Mount San Jacinto State Park Wilderness.

Right, top: Fresh footprints in the snow guide us and our oldest son through a shimmering fairyland of glittering crystalline trees — all the way to San Jacinto Peak.

Right, bottom: The summit's ice-shrouded boulders and shrubs appear just before our agreed-upon turn around time. We three are alone on San Jacinto Peak — not in the Arctic, but in Southern California, perhaps a two-hour drive from the ocean.

Below: Icy-laced branches sparkle in the sunlight two days after Christmas in Round Valley.

the Riverside Mountain Rescue Unit, Inc. told me he donates his time so that people might have another day in the mountains. "I want to keep them open, available and safe, for my son to enjoy and experience (them) as I have, and for future generations."

Forest Service volunteers work with a similar attitude. "How's it going?" volunteer Joanne Pirelli asks before checking permits. We encountered Pirelli on the popular trail from Humber Park to Tahquitz Peak. At Saddle Junction, where the trail diverges five ways, Pirelli chatted with a Scouting group. The tree-shaded junction is a good resting place for hikers who have just ascended the two-and-a-half-mile Devil's Slide Trail. Originally an 1890s cattle run, straight up the mountain to lush valleys, the trail no longer resembles its name. Today the trail includes switchbacks and views of Lily Rock, a rock-climber's haven.

On top of Tahquitz Peak, Pirelli answered visitors' questions, which pertained more to the view or the fire lookout tower than to Tahquitz. According to Cahuilla legends, this supernatural being carried people to his lair inside the mountain, never to appear again. When angry, Tahquitz made thunder and lighting.

🍂 🍂 🍂

Tahquitz Peak highlights the skyline above a revered campus meadow in the mountain village of Idyllwild. Out of respect for Native Americans, the culturally sacred meadow is off-limits. Yet its mountain backdrop complements Idyllwild Arts, the 205-acre school of music and the arts. A marble monument dedicated to campus founders Bee and Max Krone stands across from the meadow in a sequoia grove planted by Native American Atalowa. The Krones' dream, Bee wrote, "to provide an opportunity for (the) creative spirit to grow," became reality in 1950 when students began arriving on the mile-high campus in the pines.

During a morning visit in July, 2003, the hills were alive with music, dance, visual art, and drama. In A-frame huts, teen-agers practiced cellos and pianos under the direction of chamber music professionals. In a larger room, brass players rehearsed for symphonic band and orchestra

"The earth has music for those who listen,"
— GEORGE SANTANYANA

Above: Forest Service trail volunteer Joanne Pirelli answers questions and waves to visitors who have just arrived on the summit of 8,846-foot Tahquitz Peak.

Below: Lily Rock looms through a window in the trees along the Devils Backbone Trail above Humber Park. Sometimes called a more masculine-sounding Tahquitz Rock, this granite monolith near Idyllwild attracts technical rock climbers throughout Southern California.

Formerly known as ISOMATA, Idyllwild Arts is a 205-acre school of music and the arts founded in 1950 by Bee and Max Krone. This mile-high campus in the pines features an extensive summer program and year-round academy.

Below: Cued by their instructors, pre-teenagers chassé across an outdoor stage on the Idyllwild Arts campus. Dance Phenomenon, a two-week session for ages 11-13, is one of a host of summer programs for children, juniors, youth and adults.

programs. Tucked on a campus hill, youngsters in a multi-arts day program scampered for a break near the Elfs' Shelf. Pre-teenagers, cued by their instructor, chasséd across an outdoor stage. Middle-grade children were painting freestyle in a writing-and-painting course.

Children read lines and teenagers blocked scenes for theatre productions in the Holmes Amphitheater and on other outdoor stages. Overhead, parachute-like canopies undulated in the breeze, filtering light.

These images lured us back for an evening chamber music concert in the intimate Stephens Recital Hall. In the morning we had seen acclaimed pianist Edith Orloff and cellist John Walz coaching students. Now with their Pacific Trio violinist, Roger Wilkie, they played a modern Jalbert piece and a Brahms trio, music that soared sublime. The young woman seated next to me grew up overseas and spoke halting English, but together we enjoyed the music, that "common language" referred to by campus founder Max Krone.

A passion for understanding nature is the common denominator at a protected site near Lake Fulmor. Researchers, university students, and K-12 classrooms flock to the 29-acre James San Jacinto Mountains Reserve, the first of 34 undisturbed research and

Here is a 76-trombone fanfare for Max and Bee Krone, who in 1950 realized

their dream school of music and the arts. In this nurturing environment under the pines students soar, inspired by the setting and the universal language of music, art, drama, and dance.

Summer guests have included many celebrities. While on campus, Meredith Willson composed several songs for his musical The Music Man of "Seventy-six Trombones" fame. Ansel Adams taught photography workshops. (In 1958, the three-day workshops cost $10 a person. By 1960, the cost had risen to $11.50.) One summer, Alfred Eisenstadt photographed a special layout about the school for Life Magazine.

But the heart of the mountain campus rests with students — students who are teenagers, but also adults and children, age 5 and up. Students come from other countries as well as our own, in keeping with the founders' belief that the arts are universal.

"According to our way of thinking, the arts, especially music, provide the best common ground for friendly cooperation among the peoples of the world," wrote Max Krone. "Barriers of language are hard to break down, and they help to keep us from realizing that fundamentally we are all alike . . ."

"In our arts," he continued, "we all express

about the same hopes and fears, our joys and sorrows, our longings and aspirations, our daily experiences – all of those things which mean most to us. And nowhere else do we prove how much alike we are than in our songs and dances. They provide a common language we can all understand no matter in what tongue the words may be expressed."

Today more than 1,800 students live and work together in these summer programs, mostly one- and two-week workshops. Visitors appreciate some of the campus magic when they attend student performances, distinguished artist programs and festivals, or the annual Jazz in the Pines weekend.

Reaching a step further in 1987, Idyllwild Arts expanded to include the Academy, an acclaimed college preparatory boarding school for talented young artists from around the world.

Trombonists rehearsing in the summer symphonic band program are (left to right) Daniel Fremgen, Matt Karatsu, Nicole G.Valencia, Casey Kirk, Isaac Kaplan, Vikki Ashlock, Nicky Moura, Stephen Szabadi, Katherine Wittig and Amy Van Pelt. Director Jeffrey Stupin (not pictured) keeps the rhythm.

Above: Parachute-like canopies undulate in the breeze, filtering light throughout Holmes Amphitheater as children, ages 9-12, block scenes for a mini-musical theater production under direction of Johanna McKay. In late August, Holmes Amphitheater changes venue and becomes the prime setting for the annual Jazz in the Pines on the Idyllwild Arts campus.

Below: From the Tahquitz summit lookout tower deck, you can see the southern half of the San Jacintos and a panorama of distant mountains. Volunteer fire-lookout hosts keep watch here from Memorial Weekend until the first snow.

Above: Tahquitz Peak highlights the skyline above this well-known, revered meadow on the campus of Idyllwild Arts, formerly ISOMATA. Out of respect for Native Americans, the culturally sacred meadow is off-limits; yet its mountain backdrop compliments the school's program of music and the arts.

teaching habitats in the University of California's Natural Reserve System.

The James Reserve summer calendar for 2003 brought biologists to a California Wilderness Coalition workshop and global environmentalists to a Society for Conservation Geographic Information System (GIS) conclave. Longtime Director Michael Hamilton has set up a system of studying wildlife and habitat with embedded sensors and web cams connected to computers. Anyone can view live activity by visiting their website: *http://www.jamesreserve.edu*. Watching on the web can be hypnotic. Yet it reinforced last summer's Reserve visit, when from the rustic Trailfinder Lodge viewing room I watched violet-green swallows and band-tail pigeons gathered around feeders with cameras recording.

Afterward in the large meeting room, I found a surprise. Circling the walls were black and white photographs: Harry and Grace James, who donated the Reserve acreage in 1966; select members of the Western Rangers and Trailfinders, Harry James' outdoor organizations for boys; and Katherine Saubel, Cahuilla elder. The picture brought back her parting words a few months earlier, **"Take care of the land, and it will take care of you."**

Researchers, teachers and students converge at the James Reserve to study wildlife and habitat. Donated by Harry and Grace James to the University of California in 1966, this 29-acre ecological reserve near Lake Fulmor is one of 34 sites in the university's Natural Reserve System.

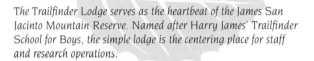

The Trailfinder Lodge serves as the heartbeat of the James San Jacinto Mountain Reserve. Named after Harry James' Trailfinder School for Boys, the simple lodge is the centering place for staff and research operations.

Everybody needs beauty as well as bread, places to play in and pray in, where nature may heal and give strength to body and soul alike.

— JOHN MUIR

Album II

Island Images

Lily Rock stands amid grandeur, connected by a saddle and broken ridge to the legendary Tahquitz Peak, as seen from the Wellman Cienega Trail. Garner Valley is visible in the distance.

It's hard not to crush these baby blue-eyes, Nemophila menziesii, on this carpet of blue when hiking up Cahuilla Mountain, but blue seems the color of this spring day. Further along the trail beyond an oak grove, the blue blossoms tangle around crystalline rocks where sprigs of maize grow nearby and boulders filled with mortar holes speak for long-ago scenes of women grinding acorns as a staple of life.

The shelter door opens on December 27, 2003. Fortunately, we don't have to use this refuge just below San Jacinto Peak, but it's nice to know it's there. Young Civilian Conservation Corps workers built the stone shelter in 1936, along with 26 miles of high country trails.

Come step through the crystalline threshold, archway to nature's magic kingdom. Moments like this live on in memory, refueling my sense of awe. Wellman Divide.

Snow plants, Sarcodes sanguinea, *always seem incongruous popping out of bare soil in early spring, like this one appearing near the trail from Saddle Junction to Tahquitz Peak.*

Ranger's buttons or swamp whiteheads, Sphenosciadium capitellatum *make a spot of summer whimsy to wet meadows and riparian areas Their rays of little flower heads brighten San Jacinto areas like Tahquitz Meadow and this Long Valley photo site.*

Shadows and sunlight play along this fern-lined path, just before
entering Tahquitz Meadow from Saddle Junction. Fern-adorned
meadows, seeping springs and seasonal wildflowers are trademarks of
many San Jacinto Mountain trails.

The pictograph remains as prehistoric evidence of the earliest known inhabitants of the San Jacintos, ancestors of the Cahuilla people. This cultural site is within a tiny Riverside County Park in Fern Valley.

Above: Melodies float through the campus trees on the Idyllwild Arts campus, as if their soulful notes could reverberate to the alpine meadows above. Here Audrey Crandell, 14, in the symphony orchestra workshop, plays a tune from the movie, Titanic.

Right: It looks like the stairway to an elf's hideaway. These granite formations in Long Valley tantalize the imagination to all who take the time to wonder.

To secure for the American people of present and future generations the benefits of an enduring resource of wilderness.
— THE WILDERNESS ACT OF 1964

Wilderness Vision

Wild places lure us yet today, thanks to countless visionary men and women. The same Harry C. James who donated his San Jacinto land for science and outdoor education worked throughout his life to preserve what is now the rugged 58,969-acre San Gorgonio Wilderness in the southeastern San Bernardino Mountains.

One of the first visions for these mountain heights is commemorated by a monument built on San Bernardino Peak in 1852, as settlers were pouring into California seeking property. Colonel Henry Washington, with only a guide, a deputy, and 11 workmen, forged through rugged terrain up the mountain with supplies to build an initial point monument, 24 feet in height. From this initial point, Washington established a north-south meridian and an east-west baseline (hence, Baseline Avenue) for surveying Southern California's land. At first glance, the monument simply looks like a pile of

One can appreciate why Colonel Washington chose this San Bernardino Peak site for the initial-point monument, establishing a north-south meridian and east-west baseline for surveying Southern California's land. Across the valley is the landmark called Slide Mountain.

rocks supporting a weathered, wooden post. But as Michael Duffy explains, "There are 6 million parcels based on this point. The peak is just a peak," he asserts. "This is a human story."

A surveyor for Metropolitan Water District, Duffy organized the Sesquicentennial Anniversary Celebration, postponed twice by fire danger and spring snow. Finally in August 2003, surveyors, friends, Boy Scouts and U.S. Forest Service representatives hiked the steep eight-mile trail from Angelus Oaks through manzanita and pines to dedicate a plaque calling attention to the nearby monument. "You're looking at the highest initial point in the US (10,290 feet), as well as the only one that has not been tampered with," Duffy said emphatically. The other 36 initial points in the western states have concrete or buildings around them. Washington's initial monument endures today, protected by the Wilderness Act of 1964. Harry James, with Joe Momyer and their Defenders of San Gorgonio Wilderness fought ski development to ensure that the Mount San Gorgonio area was included in this landmark bill.

The trail near Washington's monument on San Bernardino Peak continues eastward, weaving along a skyline ridge of 10,000-foot peaks, merging with trails coming up from different starting points, and leading ultimately to San Gorgonio's 11,499-foot summit, the highest in Southern California.

After this area received wilderness status, the Defenders formed the current San Gorgonio Wilderness Association (SGWA), whose some 125 volunteers help maintain the wilderness vision today. In July 2003, we tagged along with two of these SGWA rangers for overnight duty on the Vivian Creek Trail, a steep 8.6-mile route to San Gorgonio's summit and a popular prep-workout for hiking Mount Whitney.

Uniformed volunteers hustled in and out of Mill Creek Ranger Station's offices around 7:00 a.m. With coffee in hand, they picked up Saturday assignment sheets and radios, and then departed for designated trailheads. After assuring veterans Larry Stiles and Walter Roth that we'd hiked the Vivian Creek Trail before and that we carried a water filter and a bear barrel for storing food, we followed suit.

Near the trailhead, our party of four grew to five when the new Front Country District Ranger, Gabe Garcia, joined us. He too was using a day off, but wore his uniform like the volunteers, except with a different insignia. So now our entourage included three men in official U.S. Forest Service green.

At our first stop near Vivian Creek camp, a dozen young Scouts swarmed around the rangers, peppering them with questions. Stiles strode over to the adults resting under a tree and said "Who has the permit?" One of the fathers fished out the crumbled paper. This was the troop's first outing, he said, and the men chatted about camping etiquette and merit-badge project possibilities.

Above: "You're looking at the highest initial point in the U.S. (10,290 feet) as well as the only one that has not been tampered with," says Michael A. Duffy, speaking to the assembled entourage. A surveyor with the Metropolitan Water District, Duffy organized the event —postponed twice due to fire danger and spring snow.

Below: The entourage dedicates a plaque (#7), which the surveyors constructed beside the trail, calling attention to the initial-point monument on a short side path.

Bottom: This new plaque calls attention to Washington's initial-point monument, located up a short path.

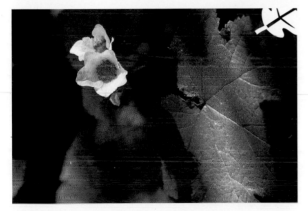

Top: Wilderness ranger Sharon Barfknecht, reaches out to greet volunteer Stiles before moving on, leading a trail crew. Barfknecht knows these mountains better than most, for she grew up coming to them with her family and Troop 1147, San Gorgonio Girl Scout Council.

Above: These thimbleberry blossoms, Rubus parviflorus, *peek out from the dense undergrowth in this shady glen near the Vivian Creek Trail Camp, a welcome relief after trudging up the steep climb from Mill Creek.*

Bottom: Clusters of hardy red Pentstemon *brighten the rocky path leading to Mill Creek and the Vivian Creek Trail.*

With variations, this scene repeated over and over all weekend, usually with an initial quick punch line from Stiles that immediately put folks at ease. Several groups had seen a bear; one party had sighted a bighorn sheep. We met young families and older adults, campers and day hikers, two more Scout groups and three flushed youths who'd just completed the Nine Peak Challenge. Two men were training to summit Mount Kilimanjaro. A Scout leader was bringing an ashen-faced, altitude-sick boy down to lower elevation. At High Creek Trail Camp, one troop had set up camp too close to the stream, so Stiles and Roth helped find new spots and move tents. A few groups didn't have correct permits, yet only one set argued fiercely before turning back. Several times we met orange-clad members of a county search-and-rescue team working on drills.

Whenever we found trees that had fallen over the trail but were too big to move, Stiles and Roth made notes for the handsaw crew. Fittingly, near the end of our weekend, we met a Forest Service trail crew carrying up a two-person saw. Stiles and Roth picked up trash, made evening rounds in the campground, and monitored their radio until 9 p.m. They resumed this activity after 7 a.m. when they stepped from their campsites looking as crisp as the day before.

"It's a fun thing to do," Stiles said, "Up here in the mountains, it's like a hobby. You do it and you enjoy it."

We enjoyed seeing the trail through their seasoned eyes. Roth pointed out wildflowers and Stiles called our attention to favorite spots. Later, as Stiles filled out forms at the Barton Flats Visitor Center, I noticed the plaque outside:

The list of founding officers includes advisory board chairman Harry James; president Joe Momyer, for whom Momyer Creek Trail is named; and secretary Alice Krueper.

Another indefatigable wilderness advocate, Krueper helped the Defenders establish the SGWA. When funding cutbacks forced the closure of Barton Flats Visitor Center, Krueper spearheaded its reopening. Staffed each summer since 1987 completely by SGWA volunteers, the Visitor Center serves thousands of visitors coming to nearby Jenks Lake, the trails, four family campgrounds, and 20 to 30 organizational camps — places that bring back first-mountain memories for a myriad of Southern California residents. Volunteers give nature walks and interpretive programs. They also serve at the Mill Creek Ranger Station and operate summer visitor centers at the Horse Meadows Historical Site and the Big Falls Picnic Area.

Some volunteers work multiple jobs. According to John Flippin, volunteer coordinator since 1993, about 80 volunteers do trail patrol on foot or horseback, while some 15 others concentrate on trail maintenance. I visited one of SGWA's required spring training meetings near Jenks Lake, where Flippin reviewed procedures and roles in the "urban wilderness."

"I always liked the mountains," Flippin told me afterward, "and it's important to be serving others."

Equestrian Coordinator Valerie Silva said she'd become a volunteer because she got caught riding up near Dollar Lake without a permit. "If you volunteer, I won't write you up," she said the Forest Service ranger told her.

"Here I am," Silva said, laughing, "21 years later."

In early summer she and two other equestrians took us on a loop to Poopout Hill near the wilderness boundary. As we rode, the volunteers visited with hikers or trimmed tree branches hanging over the trail while I admired the distant views, which looked somehow different from horseback

"If you volunteer, I won't write you up," she said the Forest Service ranger told her. "Here I am," Silva said, laughing, "21 years later."

—VALERIE SILVA

than from on foot. Yet the women didn't let me miss what was nearby — red Indian paintbrush flowers underfoot, a large doe resting beside the trail, and fresh bear tracks on the trail.

Although bears do appear in this area, I've never seen them. My surprises come more often in smaller parcels — like butterflies fluttering over yellow rabbitbrush near Hart Bar in October. This bright shrub leads to the wilderness boundary and white-barked Aspen Grove, where in the fall golden-yellow leaves quake with each breath of wind.

One summer afternoon we hiked along the Forsee Creek Trail to John's Meadow, expecting to find wildflowers there. But like other situations in life, what we expected to find at our destination, we found instead along the way. About two miles from the trailhead, past slopes of white phlox and a few Western columbine near trickling springs, the trail bent around the ridge. There, following Forsee Creek, a dazzling display of waist-high, lavender lupine waved in the breeze amid dashes of scarlet paintbrush, lemon lilies, and white, lacey cow parsnips. Closer to the water's edge, monkeyflowers and budding fireweed blended in a riot of color.

One of the original San Gorgonio Trails winds through South Fork Meadows, where innumerable springs form headwaters of the Santa Anta River. Excessive use, however, trampled the meadow's natural beauty, forcing its closure to camping in the late 1980s. The Forest Service also closed the Poopout Hill Trailhead to the meadow, lengthening the route by two-and-a-half miles and adding 1,000 feet of elevation gain. We had avoided this area in the past because of its overused reputation, but in May 2003, we found birds chirping and squirrels chattering in the regenerating meadow. SGWA volunteers Dan Scott and Mike Garant were clearing a fallen pine tree away from the trail. Still enthusiastic after 11 years' volunteering, they made their work sound like play, full of surprises.

Once on Mount San Gorgonio, Garant had discovered an historic site, the location of microwave testing in 1945 and 1946. Fourteen months later, thanks to Garant's tips, we also found the site.

Monarch butterflies hover over October's yellow rabbit brush, *Chrysothamnus nauseosus*, near Hart Bar.

This monument bears checking out

On this day, however, we continued on up through a snowy draw to find ducks bobbing on the not yet "dry" Dry Lake, which lies below the white-capped summits of San Gorgonio and surrounding peaks.

Returning to South Fork Meadow, we met backpackers on their way up. This time from the meadow we took the Dollar Lake Trail, up through pines and along a manzanita slope, which allowed some views of San Gorgonio before leading us around the ridge and then down through deep snow to the only natural lake in the wilderness. This tiny lake sits in a rocky basin, which on that day was surrounded by a silent world of snow without footprints except our own. We had to scramble up the basin's northern ridge to look down and verify that the lake glimmered like its silver dollar namesake.

Tantalized, we set off for Dollar Lake again in July of 2003 with an overnight permit and plans to summit San Gorgonio Mountain the following morning. It was muggy and hot — above 100 degrees at 3:15 p.m. — when we left our car in the parking lot near the South Fork Meadow Trailhead. Horseflies and mosquitoes swarmed about us along the trail, and in spite of swatting, I swallowed two mosquitoes before reaching the meadow. Once there, however, amid flower-fringed rivulets of water I forgot all about the pesky insects.

Dollar Lake still held a puddle of water to pump and filter, and we crawled into our sleeping bags just as the almost-full moon appeared. The temperature felt cooler when we stumbled from our tent at 4:30 a.m. with headlights guiding the way. At one point city lights twinkled below Charlton Peak's south slope. Then dawn ushered in silhouetted trees and boulders before sunrise at Dry Lake View. Pinks and oranges filled the sky and faded as mountains and the basin below came into focus.

Dollar Lake resembles its namesake, glimmering briefly like a silver dollar on this spring afternoon.

As we hiked on, the rising sun illuminated subtleties in twisted pines and trail junctions before reaching the moonscape of San Gorgonio's bare, gray back. A father-son duo met us, then a solitary man who'd camped overnight on the summit from where he'd watched six bighorn sheep grazing at sunset. When we reached the summit, a bird and a chipmunk were our only companions. Here and there, diminutive, five-needled pines sandwiched themselves between boulders. Mat-like clusters of tiny alpine flowers — pink, yellow, and blue — nestled among the windswept rocks at our feet. Up close, this summit is not truly bare, reminding me how often I overlook that which is nearby!

Above: Lemon lilies, Lilium parryi, *line the path above Forsee Creek*

Below: Golden-yellow aspen leaves quake with each breath of wind near Fish Creek and the wilderness boundary.

The rising sun at Dry Lake View, illuminates the
clouds with shades of red over the mountains in
the San Gorgonio Wilderness.

Nevertheless, I looked to the north for 10,037-foot Zahniser Peak, named after the man who authored the Wilderness Bill of 1964 and lobbied for its passage, "to secure for the American people of present and future generations the benefits of an enduring resource of wilderness."

On the trek back down the mountain we met other backpackers, day hikers, and SGWA volunteers passing along the vision. Their president, Jarome Wilson, said it best in a newsletter. He wrote that volunteer efforts add to wilderness preservation and "can plant the seed of wilderness respect . . . making a difference — today as well as tomorrow."

Right: Mat-like clusters of tiny alpine flowers nestle between the windswept boulders on the summit of Mount San Gorgonio like Erigeron compositus var. glabratus.

Below: After watching the sunrise on Mount San Gorgonio, a father and son duo head back down across the barren summit.

Opposite: A dazzling display of waist-high, lavender lupine, Lupinus polyphyllus, *wave in the breeze along Forsee Creek approaching John's Meadow.*

There are no words that can tell the hidden spirit of the wilderness, that can reveal its mystery, its melancholy and its charm.

— THEODORE ROOSEVELT
26TH PRESIDENT OF THE UNITED STATES OF AMERICA

Album III

Towering Views

Ducks bob about on Dry Lake, which often dries up by early summer.

Right, and opposite page: White prickly phlox, Leptodactylon pungen *grace the slopes along the trail to John's Meadow.*

Lower left: Dashes of scarlet Indian paintbrush, Castilleja species, *color the banks of Forsee Creek, while scarlet monkeyflowers,* Mimulus cardinalis, *cluster next to the water (lower right).*

Below: Trickling springs on the John's Meadow Trail harbor crimson columbine, Aquilegia formosa.

Falls Creek plunges some 200 feet at Big Falls, where it joins Mill Creek. The water seems to leap over the cliff from its San Bernardino Peak Divide origin, forming the highest waterfall in the San Bernardinos, as seen from a short trail near Forest Falls.

Top: San Gorgonio Wilderness Association volunteers operate a visitor center at the Horse Meadows Historical Site near Barton Flats.

Above, left: These official wilderness protectors stop on the Vivian Creek Trail to look at rings on a downed tree. From left to right, they are Walter Roth, volunteer ranger; Gabe Garcia, front country district ranger; and Larry Stiles, volunteer ranger.

Above, center: At the Barton Flats Visitors Center, a plaque dedicated on the 25th anniversary of the 1964 Wilderness Act reads "Without the Defenders, the San Gorgonio Wilderness would not exist as it does today."

Above: San Gorgonio Wilderness Association volunteers Dan Scott and Mike Garant check trail conditions during an early season patrol.

Left: Scouts pitched this tent in a legal spot at High Creek Trail Camp on the Vivian Creek Trail. Several others, however, neglected the wilderness permit regulations and set up tents in the riparian area close to the stream. So the volunteer rangers helped them find new locations.

The ridgeline from the San Bernardino Peak Divide sweeps eastward, undulating to Southern California's highest mountain, San Gorgonio.

Right: Signs like this one note the wilderness boundary, reminding us that we're entering a special area where pristine landscape, wildlife and watershed are protected, where we have space for spiritual renewal and sustainable recreation. San Bernardino Peak Trail near Angelus Oaks, San Gorgonio Wilderness.

Below: Shaped by strong wind patterns, these Jeffrey pines never fail to intrigue. No matter the year or season, they stand contorted as though the wind blows continually where they stand in an ocean of manzanita — seen when approaching the turn-off for Manzanita Springs on the San Bernardino Peak Trail.

Left: Limber pine cones and needles demonstrate their own beauty, when we take time to notice. These long-lived, stunted trees grow in dry, high ridges, as in the photo, between Dry Lake View and the summit of Mount San Gorgonio.

Below: Morning sunlight plays with shadows on this grand old incense-cedar near Vivian Creek. Vivian Creek Trail, San Gorgonio Wilderness.

Pine trees frame the massif of Old Greyback (Mount San Gorgonio) from the Momyer Creek Trail.

Above: This mountain sage, Salvia pachyphylla *belongs to late summer and the flat, sparsely wooded areas near Hart Bar Campground from Highway 38.*

Left: *The rising sun illuminates the clouds while sending sky streaks of red over the mountains from our vantage point at Dry Lake View, San Gorgonio Wilderness.*

*The world is full of beautiful places that need saving. But our Southern California forests are **our** beautiful places. These are our stomping grounds; we know these summits and canyons. If we do not work to save these natural areas, who will?*

— RALPH SALISBURY
SIERRA CLUB OUTINGS CHAIRMAN
SAN GORGONIO CHAPTER

Magnetism

"Once it's gone, it's gone," our companion said as we left Big Bear Lake's shoreline. Phil Porretta was referring to the historic marker noting the lake's original dam. His comment, however, could have applied to the wilderness, which often diminishes in direct proportion with its proximity to urban areas. Once drawing seekers of lumber, water, and gold, today this magnetic area attracts a segment of Southern California's smog-weary people searching for respite and recreation. From Crestline to Big Bear Lake, the forested crest of the San Bernardino Mountains is one of Southern California's most popular resort areas.

People flock year-round to the mountain cities clustered around Big Bear and Arrowhead Lakes — and to recreational opportunities in the surrounding national forest. Organizational campgrounds draw multi-aged visitors for multi-reasons. School groups come for outdoor education. Streams and forested mountain slopes, espe-

Summer twilight bathes Big Bear Lake in golden light, harkening back to the days of the gold rush era.

cially those free of development, enhance the allure, which diverse groups are working to protect.

Links to the area's human history entice individuals like Porretta, former member and president of the Billy Holcomb Chapter of E. Clampus Vitus, a fraternity dedicated to preserving history of the West. The local chapter's research and efforts have resulted in a number of markers registered as state historic landmarks with the California State Historic Commission. Historic landmark 725, along Big Bear Lake's southwest shoreline, notes the original 1884 dam built from hand-cut granite blocks quarried up the valley.

"When Big Bear Lake was created back in the 1880s, it was the world's largest man-made lake," Porretta said. The dam was built to supply water for Redlands' citrus groves. Yet Southern California needed more water, so the 1912 dam was built 200 yards downstream, almost doubling the lake's size.

Historic landmarks noting the mountains' treasures of lumber and gold also bear the marks of Billy Holcomb Chapter efforts. A marker west of Crestline on Hwy 18 calls attention to the Mormon Lumber Road, constructed in 1852 up through Waterman Canyon to establish sawmills on a heavily forested crest. Several markers commemorate the 1860s gold rush in Holcomb Valley.

Gold may be long gone, but its glitter remains in mining remnants and memorabilia. Last spring we set out to find some of these reminders with Porretta as guide. First stop: Big Bear Discovery Center for a self-guided auto tour pamphlet which we followed loosely in reverse order, beginning at Gold Mountain, above Baldwin Lake. Weathered remains of an ore-loading chute leaned precariously on the hillside. Once associated with a bustling mill and cyanide processing plant, the chute is not far from where the mining settlement of Bardstown (Doble) once stood. Below us stretched the dry bed of Baldwin Lake, named after Elias J. "Lucky" Baldwin, who invested in the area's last major gold discovery of 1873. His 40-stamp mill burned down in 1878, but subsequent owners built later mills.

Detouring from the auto tour, we hiked several miles to the top of Gold Mountain and followed the Pacific Coast Trail along the ridge. Pinyon pines gave way to a cluster of gigantic junipers and rosy cactus flowers as we reached the summit of multi-colored boulders. Sitting here looking south, we could see San Gorgonio's massif behind Sugarloaf Mountain with Big Bear Lake sparkling down valley.

Back on the Forest Service road we headed for Holcomb Valley, riddled with reminders of mining days. Motorcycles roared, in contrast to the silence at designated stops. Gold Fever Trail signs pointed to the place where Billy Holcomb and Ben Choteau discovered gold, to a rusted water pump from a steam-powered, five-

On the southwest shore of Big Bear Lake, a California Historical Marker notes the location of the lake's original 1884 dam, which created the world's largest man-made lake at that time.

Below: On the ridge on Gold Mountain on the Pacific Crest trail, pinyon pines give way to a cluster of gigantic, old junipers.

Bottom: Rosy blossoms of the beavertail cactus, Opuntia basilaris, come as a surprise near the 8,235 foot summit of Gold Mountain.

Weathered remains of an ore-loading chute lean precariously on the slopes of Gold Mountain above Baldwin Lake. Yellow flannelbush, *Frementodendron californicum* brightens the scene.

Above: *This quiet meadow belies Belleville's days, once filled with eager gold seekers.*

Below: *Relics of gold and silver mining, like this entrance to a tunnel blasted out of solid rock, dot Blackhawk Mountain all the way to its summit.*

stamp quartz mill, and to an arrastre, that served as the earliest gold ore grinder in the once-booming town of Belleville.

Historic markers, signs and a repositioned log cabin helped replay the 1861 scene, when 1,500 people lived in the valley, hoping to strike it rich. The registered state Holcomb Valley plaque stands outside the Big Bear Valley Historical Museum, where we ended our day, reading the marker's synopsis of Southern California's largest gold rush.

The same mountains that beguiled prospectors long ago beckon several million visitors a year, searching for recreation. Yet, away from the highways, quiet places and trails still exist where nature rules — sometimes with reminders of mining days, as on Blackhawk Mountain, northeast of Big Bear Lake. Relics of gold and silver mining dot this mountain all the way to its summit, Silver Peak.

Climbing open-forested Bertha Peak, between Bear and Holcomb Valleys, we peered down from the ridge, perhaps like Billy Holcomb did before he hunted grizzlies and discovered gold in the valley bearing his name. Southeast of Big Bear Lake, the trail climbing up 9,952-foot Sugarloaf Mountain offers intermittent views looking north through the pines to yesterday's gold-fabled mountains and today's limestone quarries. In the opposite direction, San Gorgonio Mountain rises across the Santa Ana River Canyon. Sugarloaf, shaped like its name, sits amid a roadless area that qualifies for wilderness designation — not just for nesting California spotted owls and other wildlife, but also for hikers, horseback-riders and cross-country skiers. Summer or winter, we've met few people here, whether coming from Wildhorse Creek or my favorite Green Canyon route from Big Bear.

A 110-foot, world champion lodgepole pine reigns quietly at the end of a short trail a few bumpy miles south of Big Bear Lake. From the parking area one late afternoon last summer, we followed a few family groups who set a respectful mood. They stopped to read each nature sign along the 0.3 mile path, as if on a subdued pilgrimage to the 400-year-old patriarch.

Getting to the wooded glen where Bear and Siberian Creeks merge requires a different type of pilgrimage. We chose the trail-head near Running Springs — a 2,000-feet drop, which makes the hardest part coming back up. Bear Creek is noted for its trout, but we saw no anglers or other hikers one hot Saturday morning in June. Manzanita, lupine and paintbrush lined the trail, giving way to bush monkeyflowers as we neared the stream. Crimson western columbine edged the murmuring pools, and monarch butterflies darted among branches of the overhanging trees.

Deep Creek is another dappled-lighting oasis for anglers and mountain stream lovers. We had gathered along this stream with assorted environmentalists in the spring of 2002 to celebrate senate introduction of the California Wild Heritage Bill, naming Deep Creek as a potential wild and scenic river. With headwaters in Running Springs, the creek becomes the east fork of the Mojave River flowing to the desert. In places, the water tumbles between pools below rocky cliffs.

A year later, we returned to the same area northeast of Cedar Glen, but this time I plopped down beside a quiet pool with tall green grasses and just listened to the sound of water. A bird kept calling down, down, down the scale. When I looked up at a ledge around the bend, I could see the shoes and a hat of a nameless person resting in the sunshine.

Earlier that morning, I'd watched energetic school children learning outdoors in nearby Lake Arrowhead. "Hey, you," a naturalist called out.

"Who, me?" responded about two dozen sixth graders checking out trees at Arrowhead Ranch Outdoor Science School.

"Yeah, you," the naturalist countered.

"What's uuuuup?" shouted the children on cue as they gathered around.

"What's this?" the naturalist asked, holding up a yellow pine's three-needle bundle. "Bend it here, and it makes a Y."

Hands shot up with the correct answer, and we moved on with the vivacious director and CEO Kathy Farley. Since 1957, school children have been coming for a week's outdoor education to Ar-

Meet George & Gracie and Luci & Desi.
These couples are nesting bald eagles who keep returning each winter around the shores of Big Bear Lake. Bald eagles migrate here for several months, and signs go up in certain locations reading, "Closed. Eagle habitat: Do not enter. Closed from Dec. 1 to Mar. 31."

Savvy area residents, however, recognize some of the returning eagles, like the above pairs, who perch in familiar, visible spots. Volunteers at the Discovery Center keep a telescope fixed on one eagle perch. They also operate two-hour eagle tours. For prices and dates, call the Big Bear Discovery Center at 909-866-3437.

Above: Todd Murphy, Chairman of the Discovery Center Advisory Board, holds up the famous bald-eagle picture on one of the Center's brochures.

Shaped like its namesake, Lake Arrowhead is a magnetic center for mountain tourism and retreat, offering scores of educational and recreational opportunities.

The National Children's Forest trail calls to the child in each of us.

Children's whimsical artwork decorates signposts; landmarks named Pillow Rock or Chipmunk Condo bring out the smiles. But the ¾-mile wheelchair-accessible trail is only one aspect of the Children's Forest.

Programs are ongoing throughout the year, although concentrated in the summer when about 80 volunteers, ages 11 to 17, lead nature walks along the trail, staff the visitor information center and supervise activities like making paw-print casts. They also present nature programs and slideshows at public lakefront locations or campgrounds.

"Kids make it. This is their place," says Cheryl Nagy, program coordinator. Youth volunteers helped design the nature trail, consistent with National Children's Forest focus on youth development and conservation education. The Visitor Information Center is located on California 18 at the turnoff for Keller Peak Fire Lookout, another worthwhile destination within the Children's Forest.

Above: A little girl reads pictures on the whimsical sign describing Pillow Rock in the National Children's Forest near Keller Peak.

rowhead Ranch outdoor science school, initially known as Camp O-ongo near Running Springs. Farley began working there in 1994, first as an administrative assistant, but soon in every capacity. "I fell in love with the company and idea in the first month there," she said. "What a great change it made in these kids."

When financial and other difficulties threatened closure, Farley bought the school and turned it around, operating from area church conference grounds. In 2003, she secured funding sources to buy the former Ice Castle International Training Center, which still maintains a practice rink on the property. "This is the place," Farley said, showing us proudly around the school's new permanent home.

"We are visitors. We are guests here (in the forest)" she said they tell the children. Through hands-on activities and games that replicate animal experiences, the students learn about ecology and "saving our forests."

The lakes area is flush with organizational campgrounds and facilities of varying focus and mountain perspective. Katy Council remembers "enjoying the great outdoors" at YMCA Camp Oakes near Big Bear City. "It was a very important time in my life," Council said, commenting on her experiences first as a young camper, then as a leadership trainee, and finally as counselor leading others in skits, team-building activities, and inspirational ceremonies.

"The whole camp is an outdoor setting," she said, reminiscing about three-wall cabins and smelling the trees. "I really think that that had a lot to do with why I love the wilderness now." A public school teacher, Council likes getting away from Southern California's "concrete land" and visiting the mountains "to smell the clean air and pine trees."

Protecting this mountain resource is key to a growing number of group efforts. More than 600 volunteers work in partnership with the U.S. Forest Service under the San Bernardino National Forest Association (SBNFA) umbrella, organized in 1992, "to preserve the forest for the enjoyment of visitors . . . " Some 130 of these volunteers do interpretive work, give tours, and operate the expanding Big Bear Discovery Center near Fawnskin. About 30 volunteers oversee youth at the National Children's Forest, a 3,400-acre educational site east of Running Springs.

Fire Lookout Hosts serve at seven lookout towers from Memorial Day until the first snow. They also work at the restored Morton Peak Lookout when it's not rented by guests. About 300 trained volunteers rotate hours, scanning for smoke and lightning strikes every 15 minutes during daytime shifts. If hosts stay overnight — and no forest fires are burning — evenings are free. That's when

Right: Shoes and hat, belonging to a nameless sun worshiper, stick out on a rocky ledge around the bend from the author's Deep Creek resting place.

six-year veterans Cindy and Gary Weber enjoy watching the sunset. "We love the outdoors and want to help protect it," Cindy says.

Forest caring groups not associated with SBNFA include the Friends of Fawnskin, Pacific Coast Trail Association, and Rim of the World Interpretive Association, better known as Heaps Peak Arboretum. This latter group has cooperated with the Forest Service since 1982, providing education programs and facilities.

The Wildlands Conservancy, based at its Oak Glen Preserve, continues acquiring private land within the national forests to preserve them from urban encroachment. The San Bernardino Mountains Land Trust, Save Our Forests Association, and Mountain Rim Fire Safe Council strive to preserve these mountains and prevent devastating fires.

Environmental groups, such as the Audubon Society, Center for Biological Diversity and Sierra Club, work actively throughout these mountains. The Sierra Club sponsors outings to acquaint others with our mountains' beauty, while working to preserve their scenic views, the land itself, and its wildlife.

"The world is full of beautiful places that need saving," writes Ralph Salisbury, Sierra Club Outings Chair, San Gorgonio Chapter. "But our Southern California forests are *our* beautiful places. These are our stomping grounds; we know these summits and canyons. If we do not work to save these natural areas, who will?"

Top: At Arrowhead Ranch outdoor science school naturalist Alison Bates points out features of nearby trees to energetic but attentive sixth graders.

Above: Volunteers staff the Keller Peak Fire Lookout Tower, and the other forest lookouts, from Memorial Day until the first snowfall.

Below: It's a bridge over still waters. But not too far away where the gorge narrows, Deep Creek tumbles over large boulders and forms deep pools.

Sun-dappled shade and the sound of tumbling water near the
merger of Bear and Siberia Creeks offer a welcome respite
on a hot day in late June.

The trail is beautiful . . . be still.

— LAKOTA PROVERB

Album IV

Rim Reflections

As you round the bend on Highway 38 near Onyx Pass, the massif of Mount San Gorgonio unfolds before you.

Above: A quiet pool edged by green grasses is a perfect place to rest, reflect, and listen to the sound of flowing water.

Left: Taking a leap of faith, John Monsen jumps over the arm of a pool on Deep Creek.

Opposite: A series of deep pools interrupt Deep Creek's flow, making perfect places to fish, sit on a ledge or listen for birds.

Above: A cross-country skier takes a break on a mild winter day near Onyx Pass. Only the intermittent swish of skis breaks the silence of the forest.

Right: Snow around Onyx Pass gives an opportunity to explore the winter world on snowshoes or cross-country skis.

The sylvan area where Bear Creek merges with Siberia Creek is a popular destination for hikers as well as trout anglers. But sometimes, you may not find anyone else around.

Top: Phil Poretta rereads the words that he researched and wrote for this state registered Holcomb Valley plaque that stands outside the Big Bear Valley Historical Museum.

Center: This site looks inconspicuous, but the Gold Fever Trail sign points out the meadow where Billy Holcomb and Ben Choteau discovered gold near a seasonal stream.

Bottom: The Gold Fever Trail self-guided auto tour includes the remains of the pygmy cabin, so-named, because its door was barely four-feet high, and its roof peaked only six-feet above the floor before it burned down.

Top: Timbers left from the gold mining days frame San Gorgonio as they lean precariously on the summit of Gold Mountain.

Left: A rusted water pump is all that remains of this steam-powered, five-stamp mill in Holcomb Valley.

Above: Used for grinding rock to remove gold, this arrastre is in the Belleville town site. At one time miners used arrastres like these throughout Holcomb Valley.

Colorful Indian paintbrush and other wildflowers near this tree stump
look as if arranged by a divine florist, on the Bear Creek Trail.

Top: In mid-June, these pink wooly bluecurls, Trichostema lanatum *bloom amid the chaparral on the Bear Creek Trail near Running Springs.*

Above: These silver puffs, Uropappus lindleyi, *sparkle like glass crystals on a stick.*

Above: Which beguiles more along Bear Creek, the crimson western columbine, Aquilegia Formosa or the quiet pool reflecting a blue sky?

Right: One species of Utah's state flower, the mariposa-lily, Calochortus, seems to grow out of the rocks in the Bear Creek drainage area.

Opposite: Perky bush, or sticky, monkeyflowers, Mimulus aurantiacus, gives us a lift wherever they appear, as on the slopes approaching Bear Creek.

Baldy Prospects

A Nelson Bighorn Sheep stood on the trail about 20 to 30 feet away, and Will Vanderwilt froze. "I could see his eyes; we looked at each other," Vanderwilt said, remembering that summer morning back in the mid-1970s. It was probably only 15 seconds before the sheep bolted, he said, but then a herd followed, "like they were coming out of the rocks . . . and they were moving pretty fast." He lost count, but estimated that 50 sheep crossed his path. When the procession ended, Vanderwilt proceeded to the top of 10,064-foot Mount San Antonio, musing about his "once in a lifetime experience" on a little-used back route from Upper Fish Fork out of Blue Ridge.

Rare at the time, this scene is virtually impossible today. According to the California Department of Fish and Game (CDFG)'s count of March 2004, the total Nelson Bighorn Sheep population

Mount San Antonio, better known as Old Baldy or Mount Baldy, is the Los Angeles area's signature mountain, highest in the San Gabriels. Its summit glistens in midwinter sunshine, a magnificent sight from afar or from the Timber Mountain Trail above Icehouse Saddle as in this photo.

The Nelson Bighorn Sheep are

classified as the Cucamonga Peak, Mount San Antonio, Iron Mountain and Twin Peak herds. A herd population below 100 is not considered sustainable.

Above: Belonging to the Mount San Antonio herd, this bighorn sheep darts within view below Baldy Notch before disappearing again in the forest.

in the San Gabriel Mountains has dwindled to 157 sheep — from about 500 to 700 in the 1970s and 1980s. Consequently, the U.S. Forest Service, Los Angeles County Fish and Game Commission, and CDFG are working on a project to restore these sheep to a viable population.

The proximity of these mountains to our burgeoning megapolis adds to the challenge of maintaining wildlife habitat, watershed, and healthy forests in balance with human needs for respite and recreation. From Mount San Antonio's summit to the surrounding canyons and peaks, a groundswell of concern is building — to care for these "fountains of life" that John Muir extolled.

Mount San Antonio (called Old Baldy or Mount Baldy) is the greater Los Angeles area's signature mountain, highest in the San Gabriel range, visible from many parts of Southern California. Its bare (bald), rounded summit looks white even when not covered with snow, and it beckons us to admire from afar or seek out its foothills, canyons, and streams. Its accessibility and challenging routes of about 4,000-feet elevation gain to the summit make it one of the area's most frequently hiked mountains. Old Baldy attracts extreme hikers, training to climb some of the world's highest peaks, as well as others who shorten their route by riding the ski lift to Baldy Notch.

Summit tales are private and legendary. For a few, it's the Labor Day Baldy Run to the Top, or the Annual Baldy Peaks 50K with two runs to the summit. For others, it's an annual moonlight hike to the top, or discovering the exposed Devil's Backbone Ridge in daylight after negotiating it in darkness the night before. Once, along this ridge, a friend pointed out violet-green swallows and white-throated swifts swooping and gliding in the wind.

I like the summit view on clear days when you can see the panorama of mountains, ocean and desert. At least once I saw the Sierra Nevada's southern edge. There's a common exhilaration on top, which the first recorded climbers in the late 1800s must have felt, or the guests that mountain guide William Dewey brought up to his Baldy Summit Inn during the summers of 1910-1912. My husband marvels that we are close to 15 million people, yet up above in a different world by ourselves. Usually we're not alone, but share the view — and rocky windbreaks — with friends and strangers from around the globe.

Sometimes, when taking the San Antonio Canyon route to the top, we see one or two Nelson Bighorn Sheep in the Baldy Bowl or among spring-fed wildflowers near the San Antonio Ski Hut. Last summer we veered off this trail to check out foundations of the 1897-vintage Gold Ridge Mine, but a rattlesnake shooed us away.

Gold. This glittery discovery in upper San Antonio Canyon and on Baldy Notch brought prospectors, entrepreneurs and pioneers, whose tales live on in Baldy lore. A month after our snake encounter

On a clear day in the Los Angeles Basin the skyline of the San Gabriel's beckons us to admire, or to seek out its foothills, canyons and streams.

near Gold Ridge Mine, we walked in miners' territory along Baldy Notch as part of a Sierra Club outing with historian and author John Robinson. He led us to a former Hocamac Mining Company site, which he identified by trees shown in a mid-1890s photograph of a hydraulic mine set-up. To get enough water, the company built a two-mile pipeline from San Antonio Creek's headwaters, Robinson said. But the hydraulic system's waste water polluted the creek downstream, which forced limited operations and made their mining ventures ultimately unprofitable.

Perhaps some of those pictured miners purchased supplies at Dell's Camp, before its brief resort days near today's trout pools In Mount Baldy Village. On private property below are remnants of Camp Baldy's open-air dance pavilion, built when Foster and Ruth Curry expanded their popular resort across the creek — before the devastating 1938 flood. Reminders of another resort are evident above today's village in Icehouse Canyon — with foundations and many remaining fireplaces built by pioneer Clarence Roy Chapman, who brought his family here in 1913. Later he built the Chapman Ranch, where his son Bob lives with his wife Pat, who started the Chapman Ranch School.

Since 1980, school children and teachers throughout the greater Los Angeles area have made yearly pilgrimages here for hands-on learn-

From Mount San Antonio's summit to the surrounding canyons and peaks, a groundswell of concern is building — to care for these "fountains of life" that John Muir extolled.

ing in a natural environment with Pat Chapman and her staff.

Former student Travis Huxman had an advantage by living in Mount Baldy Village, feeling part of the Ranch School until he was in high school. "It taught me that I could do anything I tried. It gave me the confidence," said Huxman, assistant professor, ecology and evolutionary biology, University of Arizona.

Last summer we visited this innovative school, and even though no classrooms or teachers-in training were present that day, the grounds reverberated with director Chapman's learning activities around the bird and bee hive observatories, vegetable garden, animal barn, school barn, hiking trails, pond, sundial and Native American shelters. The Ranch School inspiration, she said, came from Harry James.

Training teachers is Chapman's focus these days, along with showing park or visitor center naturalists how to build natural learning areas within the urban environment. "Environment can't be something you're always going away to," said Chapman, a public school teacher before opening the mountain school. "It's got to be around you and that's where you learn to love it."

Alongside Chapman, her husband Bob has used the ranch saw-mill, forge and adapted recycled items to build almost anything their school and home needed. Similarly, he built the 1949 addition to the old schoolhouse, now the Mount Baldy Visitor Center. A plaque there pays tribute to his inventive structures and "vivid accounts" of the San Antonio Canyon area, his beloved home and environment.

Trails — like the legends of pioneers, entrepreneurs and prospectors — radiate beyond Old Baldy from Icehouse Saddle, Lytle Creek, and the Blue Ridge areas to the valley foothills. One of the most heavily used trails follows Icehouse Canyon about four miles to Icehouse Saddle. One of my favorite stories from John Robinson's *The San Gabriels* explains how Icehouse Canyon supposedly got its name, from blocks of canyon ice packed by mules and wagons down to the valley below. The earliest report dates back to 1858 when Los Angeles residents made ice cream using canyon ice.

Families play near the crystal-clear creek in the lower part of this boulder-strewn canyon where wildflowers bloom in season. We've brought out-of- town friends here to frolic in the snow, or once, to admire the venerable incense cedars in fog. A side loop, called the Chapman Trail, passes through Cedar Glen, another stand of these majestic trees.

Most times, however, we follow the trail to the saddle. The 2,600 foot climb is steep, especially past the Cucamonga Wilderness sign, but I like the rhythm of my feet on the trail and the sound of wind blowing through the tall pines overhead just below the saddle. This scenic junction of four trails is always a good resting point, where sometimes we've seen hikers approaching from the Middle Fork of Lytle Creek to the east. But we either turn around here or take one of the other three trails — to Timber Mountain, which continues on to Telegraph Peak and Thunder Mountain, the popular 3T's hike; to Ontario Peak, via Kelly's Camp 1922 foundations and scarred, lodgepole pine survivors of the 1980 fire; or our favorite, southeast, to 8,859-foot Cucamonga Peak where you can look down on familiar valley landmarks with the San Bernardino and San Jacinto Mountains in the distance.

Top: On summer weekends, the summit of Mount Baldy can look crowded. In fact, this peak is Southern California's most frequently climbed mountain, due to its accessibility in the greater Los Angeles area and its challenging routes of about 4000-feet elevation gain. In the foreground, Ralph Glenn looks up for a glider plane. Waiting obediently is his dog Tenzing Norgay, named after a member of the first party to summit Mount Everest.

Second from top: In this silhouette, David Thorne hikes the Ski-Hut Trail, one of many routes to Baldy's summit. The mountain attracts extreme hikers training to climb some of the world's highest peaks, while others shorten the climb by taking the chairlift to Baldy Notch.

Third from top: Exposure on both sides of the Devil's Backbone adds to the fun factor on this popular route to Mount Baldy's summit.

Bottom: On a clear day from the summit of Mount Baldy, a hiker's reward is the 360-degree panorama of mountains, desert and ocean. Here two hikers share the view and a rocky wind break on Mount Baldy's summit.

Wildflower "gardens" thrive in the seeps and springs near the San Antonio Ski Hut below Baldy Bowl. Orange-splashed Bigelow's sneezeweed, *Helenium bigelovii*, dominates in the foreground.

Above: This fireplace stands as a reminder of former years, before the devastating 1938 flood destroyed many cabins in Icehouse Canyon as well as Camp Baldy in Mount Baldy village. Pioneer Clarence Roy Chapman built many fireplaces in the area.

Right: The entire Chapman Ranch and School speak of Bob Chapman's ingenuity. Using the ranch forge, sawmill, and adapted recycled items; Bob Chapman built everything they needed.

Below: The old Mount Baldy schoolhouse, with a 1949 addition built by Bob Chapman, is now part of the Mount Baldy Visitor Center.

Vanderwilt said his children always looked forward to an annual backpacking trip to Cucamonga Peak. After a night there, they'd descend eastward for a second night near the Joe Elliott Tree (before the giant sugar pine was removed) and on to San Sevaine Flats for a car shuttle home.

The northeastern edge of the San Gabriel Mountains contains some of the range's most rugged wilderness and spectacular scenery. With deep canyons and sharp ridges, the peaks appear grander and somewhat formidable, plunging to the San Andreas Fault where the range ends. Of the many natural scenic areas here, three are special for me.

Cascading water and clear pools draw anglers and hikers to the Middle Fork of Lytle Creek. Eating lunch one spring Saturday with friends near Third Stream Crossing, we watched two little birds fighting over another — just before a young Scout group approached to set up a wilderness camp. Earlier, near a tributary stream cascading down the gorge, we had met an older Scout group headed up toward Icehouse Saddle. Here again eight months after the Grand Prix Fire of 2003, we met a happy but tired young man who had rappelled down the tributary canyon waterfalls.. He'd driven here from San Jose, specifically for this adventure.

Several years ago we caught the Stockton Flat area on a rare, crystalline wintry day and made the first human footprints alongside rabbit tracks in the snow. I hugged a snowy tree and felt like dancing in those surreal moments, silent except for my boots' sinking into the snow. Sometimes I just stood and gaped at this pristine setting so close to home. The snow-covered Devil's Backbone Trail, leading up Mount Baldy from the Notch, looked even more impressive from down below than when hiking it up above.

Last spring, friends urged us to hike a non-maintained route, the North Devil's Backbone Trail up Pine Mountain to the north ridge of Mount Baldy. Flowers filled the approaching walk. Mountain views seemed more dramatic the further we climbed — from the Blue Ridge Road to the steep razorback ridge, up and down Pine Mountain, up and around Dawson Peak to a stunning panorama ridge view. From this vantage point, hikers on Mount Baldy looked like ants moving up the more popular Devil's Backbone Trail from Baldy Notch. We turned around here because of too much snow on Baldy's steep north ridge. The few people we met that day seemed to take special pride in the area, an attitude I saw repeated by others in Old Baldy's domain.

❦ ❦ ❦

"Poachers," he said, pointing to an empty bleach bottle trashed beside the stream. "They come here and dump a bottle of cheap bleach, or sometimes ammonia, in the stream. It suffocates the fish and they float to the top, where the poacher scoops them up with a net or something." Bill Reeves was showing us a section of

Above: Scarlet monkeyflowers, Mimulus cardinalis, *perch beside an incense-cedar log above the stream in lower Icehouse Canyon.*

Right: The Icehouse Canyon trail is steep when approaching the saddle, but intermittent views of Mount Baldy more than compensate for the effort.

Below: Hikers take a break at Icehouse Saddle before taking one of four different trails that radiate from this scenic junction.

Trout in the Classroom is making waves.

Reeves works also with this program, sponsored locally by the Federation of Fly Fishers. Upon teachers' requests, volunteers take trout eggs to area-school classrooms, K-12, sometimes for science, but also for art, math, or any other subject.

The students must build a cover for their aquaria to protect the eggs from fluorescent light and take care of the hatched fish until they're ready to be released. Volunteers then accompany each class to a mountain stream for releasing the fish, where the students learn about stream entomology, fish history, and fly-casting.

Reeves estimates that his local club reaches 2,500 students a year, as do other Fly Fisher units throughout Southern California. Conservation groups across the U.S. and Canada are sponsoring Trout in a Classroom projects, teaching young people in the process to protect and conserve stream habitat.

Above: San Antonio Creek is one of the mountain streams where volunteers accompany school groups to release trout, hatched in their classrooms. This final event is part of the Trout in the Classroom program sponsored by the Federation of Fly Fishers.

Above: Poachers! They pour bleach into the water, as this bottle testifies on San Antonio Creek. The bleach then suffocates and kills the fish.

Below: Bill Reeves, Fisheries Resource Volunteer Corps executive director, tells how 40 empty bleach bottles were picked up in one day along a section of this stream.

San Antonio Creek, one of the mountain streams that the Fisheries Resource Volunteer Corps strives to preserve.

One fisheries crew picked up 40 empty bleach bottles along that stream in one day, and "that's pretty sad," Reeves said, shaking his head. However, mountains streams are cleaner, showing less vandalism since local fly fishermen initiated their program under the auspices of the Federation of Fly Fishers in 1994.

About 100 trained, uniformed volunteers monitor and protect mountain streams, educating people along the way. Although volunteers pick up trash and clean graffiti — using an efficient water blaster when terrain allows — public contact is the most important work they do, according to Reeves, executive director. He said their presence in uniform makes a big difference. They routinely hand out trash bags and talk about preserving the area while serving as eyes for the government groups who work with the Fisheries Corps. The Forest Service helps with uniforms, radios and training. Begun along Deep Creek in the San Bernardino Mountains, the program now includes Bear and City Creeks, Santa Ana River, Lytle Creek, San Antonio Creek, East and West Fork of the San Gabriel River, and Piru Creek.

Volunteers and non-profit groups are working with government entities in countless other ways, such as the project addressing the San Gabriel Mountains' diminishing Nelson Bighorn Sheep, classified as a sensitive species by the U.S. Forest Service. According to Gabe Garcia, front country district ranger, San Bernardino National Forest (SBNF), the project is looking at habitat, predation, and human impact. "We're glad that we've got a management plan coming together," Garcia said. The eastern end of the San Gabriels is within Garcia's district and the bighorn sheep is SBNF's logo. "If this management plan is successful," Garcia quipped, "I get to keep the sheep on my business card."

Volunteers assist U.S. Forest Service staff and ranger Rick Dean, who for five years has coordinated a year-round nature center at the Mount Baldy Visitor Center where about 8,000 schoolchildren a year learn about the environment, geology, and history. Eagle Scout projects focus regularly on the Baldy area, more than 20 a year repairing sections of the Icehouse Canyon Trail. Mountain volunteer organizations are proliferating, with mind-boggling types of service.

In the foothills, residents are working to prevent urban sprawl from intruding into the canyons. For example, Friends of Day Canyon helped protect that lovely canyon's watershed and wildlife from development. The Claremont Wildlands Conservancy is working to preserve open space known as Johnson's Pasture in the foothills above Claremont. Caring for these "fountains of life" that Muir wrote about suggests new prospects for Old Baldy's expansive domain.

Cascading water and clear pools draw anglers, hikers, and picnickers to the Middle Fork of Lytle Creek, an area qualifying for wilderness protection.

A stroll through Johnson's Pasture just before sundown illustrates why the Claremont Wildlands Conservancy is working to preserve this compelling open space in the foothills above Claremont.

The lovely waterfall near the mouth of Day Canyon remains pristine,
partially through the efforts of the Friends of Day Canyon.

This scene taken several years ago from Etiwanda shows Cucamonga Peak looking out over the foothills bordering Rancho Cucamonga, where groups are working to protect the canyons from urban encroachment.

During the dedication of the Tongva village, three women dancing "The Circle of Life," are, from left to right, Feather Woman, Arlene Morales and Two Moon Woman. The standing male with his back to the camera is Guiding Young Cloud, and the seated male to the far right is Firehorn. According to Tongva elder Mark Acuña, they are working at Mount Baldy (Joatngna) for cultural renewal and tribal celebration. Volunteer work to construct the village reproduction, begun in 1999, includes Forest Service personnel, Boy Scouts and their families, tribal members and friends.

History comes alive at the Mount Baldy Visitor Center. Dedication

of the Native American Tongva (Gabrielino) village in June of 2004 was part of the San Gabriel Mountains history series, primarily for adults, sponsored by the U.S. Forest Service. The reproduced village, with its thatched hut, granary, and ceremonial house and fire ring, is used in the center's Environmental Education Program. Close by is a replica of a gold camp, where elementary children use sluice boxes "to find gold."

O these vast, calm, measureless mountain days....
Days in whose light everything seems equally
divine, opening a thousand windows to show us
God.

— JOHN MUIR

Album V

Scenic
Signatures

Across the drainage from Lytle Creek Ridge, Mount Baldy and its neighbors reign supreme.

Above: Day Canyon remains special to Al and Dot Rhodes, because their daughter, Kim, was one of the Chaffey College students who worked with others to preserve the canyon's watershed and wildlife for future generations.

Opposite: A Wilderness Travel Group practices snowshoeing on one of their mountain events near Wrightwood.

Above: A procession of hikers begins the steep climb from beneath Baldy Bowl to Mount Baldy's summit.

Right: An easy walk from Baldy Road at Manker Flats, San Antonio Falls is popular with all ages and familiar to hikers going on to the top of Mount Baldy.

Tales of adventure stem from Baldy Bowl, as seen here from the Icehouse Canyon Trail. When snow conditions are right, hardy skiers carry skis on their back to the top of the bowl for the next run down.

The south side of Cucamonga Peak drops dramatically towards Deer Canyon and the Inland
Valley below, while San Jacinto Peak rises above the haze on the horizon.

Looking south from the top of Cucamonga Peak, the Inland Valley spreads out below, with
the familiar shape of Old Saddleback and the Santa Ana Mountains in the distance.

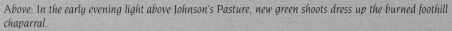

Above: In the early evening light above Johnson's Pasture, new green shoots dress up the burned foothill chaparral.

Right: The image of Mount Baldy and its associated peaks draws us in, from the mouth of historic San Antonio Canyon's portal to the grandeur above.

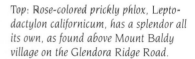

Top: Rose-colored prickly phlox, Lepto-dactylon californicum, has a splendor all its own, as found above Mount Baldy village on the Glendora Ridge Road.

Center: Wildflowers like these lupine, Lupinus excubitus, fill the hillsides, appearing around almost every corner of the trail on the approach to Pine Mountain near Wrightwood.

Bottom: The orange-colored Bigelow's sneezeweed, Helenium bigelovii, brightens mountain gardens, as in this spring-fed oasis near the San Antonio Ski Hut.

Opposite: Pink Ceanothus nestles beside the stately California juniper on the slopes above Mt. Baldy village.

Above left: This burned-out lodgepole pine near Ontario Peak stands as a silent reminder of the ravaging 1980 fire.

Left: Looking like ghostly fingers, the bleached branches of a dead manzanita reach out from patches of rabbitbrush, Chrysothamnus nauseosus, on the Devil's Backbone Trail.

Above: Hikers look like ants on the popular Devil's Backbone Trail, when looking from Dawson Peak towards the north ridge of Mount Baldy.

I will lift up mine eyes unto the hills from whence cometh my help.

— PSALMS 121:1, THE HOLY BIBLE
KING JAMES VERSION

Living Treasures

Every fall, extreme runners throughout the U.S. converge for an ultimate challenge — the Angeles Crest 100. This grueling 100-mile mountain race begins in Wrightwood, and after a mind-boggling 48,000 vertical feet gained and lost, ends in Pasadena. The route threads up, down and around much of the scenic, historic San Gabriel Mountains — mountains that inspire valley residents looking up, and in September, 2003, we watched part of this annual mountain race.

7 a.m. Two hours after the race begins, we join other cars at mile 13.85, Vincent Gap, and wait for the lead runners to come through. As support crew friends and families start laying out supplies, I replay my visit to Vincent Gap three months earlier.

From the Gap we'd walked down the old wagon-road trail to the stamp-mill ruins of Big Horn Mine. Along the way, red soil and yellow-blooming flannel bushes framed the eastern vista of Mount

Snowcapped summits glisten on a sparkling April morning from this view point on Highway 39 near Morris Reservoir.

Runners head up the ridge toward 9,399 foot Mount Baden-Powell in the grueling Angeles Crest 100-mile mountain race. After negotiating some 40 switchbacks uphill from Vincent Gap, they bypass the actual summit and turn downhill toward Little Jimmy campground.

Baldy and nearby peaks. We crossed a talus slope, maneuvered our way through washouts in the road, then veered around the corner and stopped. Ahead, on the eastern slopes of Mount Baden Powell, nestled the remains of an ore-processing mill.

There weren't any "no trespassing" signs, so we poked around for a few minutes. The only sounds came from a streamlet of water trickling under a wooden catwalk; the only life, a lizard, sunning itself on the mill's foundation, facing the mountains above the San Gabriel Canyon far below.

Charles Tom Vincent, after whom Vincent Gap is named, discovered gold here in 1894. But the 10-stamp mill and wagon road were built by later owners during the more profitable early 1900s. Reportedly, exploratory work still takes place here now and then.

7:08 a.m. People start clapping as the front runner passes by the first aid station and crosses the highway to the Vincent Gap parking lot. He stops only long enough to down a cup of fluid while a young woman straps a Camelback over his shoulders. Then

We wind on up to the summit where the racers below look like toy figures playing in front of a magnificent backdrop.

he's on his way, up the Mount Baden-Powell trail. Soon other runners follow. One slender male grabs a handful of cookies, then a bunch of chips and a few orange slices before heading on up the steep trail in a fast walk. We follow along during a lull, getting out of the way when more runners come by. I don't count, but literature claims 41 switchbacks in four miles. This popular CCC-constructed trail reaches Mount Baden-Powell's 9,399-foot summit after an elevation gain of 2,800 feet.

8:30 a.m. About two switchbacks below the peak, we stop beside a contorted, 1,500-year-old limber pine, and watch runners parade across the ridge saddle. An AC100 race alumnus photographs runners as they cross the saddle and head down the Pacific Coast Trail toward Little Jimmy Campground. We wind on up to the summit where the racers below look like toy figures playing in front of a magnificent backdrop. In the canyon far below, I recognize the East Fork of the San Gabriel River, upstream from the Bridge to Nowhere, where we'd hiked in the spring.

The old wagon road leading to the Big Horn Mine offers stunning views — flannelbush gold before deep canyons of the Sheep Mountain Wilderness extending to Mount Baldy and the surrounding peaks.

9 a.m. Before heading back down, we wander over to the Boy Scout Monument built in 1957. Scouts make an annual 53-mile Silver Moccasin trek from Chantry Flat to this peak named for their founder, Lord Baden-Powell. Their route, and the Silver Moccasin Trail, is part of the AC100's next 50 miles. We follow the race no further, but recognize many sites along this stretch. From Baden-Powell, the course continues past other peaks, Windy Gap and Islip Saddle (mile 26) to Cooper Canyon.

Many years ago Ron Huxman, special agent, San Bernardino National Forest, lived and worked at remote Buckhorn National Forest Ranger Station near Cooper Canyon. The station has been torn down, but the loop from Buckhorn Campground through Cooper Canyon and back to Highway 2 remains as Huxman described.

"It's an absolutely gorgeous, pristine hike," he'd said.

We tried it one Saturday in late April after the snow had melted. Statuesque incense cedars gleamed as if pointing the way to a beautiful waterfall near the fork where trails meet. Someone had tied a strong rope to a sturdy pine tree, making a handhold to drop down the slippery, steep stream bank to the waterfall's pool, where sparkling spray muted the light patterns on the surrounding cliffs and trees. Later, up the canyon, clusters of pale-pink manzanita blossoms nodded in the cold wind, while fuzzy willow catkins looked translucent in the late afternoon sun.

Racers continue from Cooper Canyon to Mount Hilyer, Chilao (a hideout for Tiburcio Vasquez's bandido gang) and Shortcut Saddle, the AC-100's 59-mile point. Our friend Brian Elliott, an AC100 finisher in 1995, said at the Saddle first-aid station, one group gave the runners ice cream. It was about midnight for him. "I liked the nighttime," he said, "with all the insects making noises in the woods." About 1 a.m., however, after West Fork and on the downhill stretch from Newcomb's Saddle, all he wanted to do was stop for a minute and sleep. The race continues through Big Santa Anita Canyon near 50-foot Sturtevant Falls, but for safety reasons, veers away.

I didn't want to sleep last May when we walked up that canyon, but I felt like lingering at Sturtevant Falls and listening to the music of the water. Wildflower blossoms and smells were equally compelling, so much so that we didn't get as far up as Sturtevant's Camp of the 1890s. Blame it on those wild Canterbury bells.

Two miles below the falls, racers reach the 75- mile-point, Chantry Flat, where pacers can join them. Then they begin climbing up Mount Wilson. Continuing with a leg injury, Elliott said this segment of the race was his most difficult, yet the sunrise as he neared the mountain top was one of the nicest parts.

Chantry Flat is the starting point for several interlocking routes to hike up Mount Wilson. Native Americans established the first footpath up the mountain, and in 1864, Benjamin Wilson built the first modern trail to log timber. His route, the Old Mount Wilson Trail through Little Santa Anita Canyon above Sierra Madre, soon

Above: It comes into view as you round the corner of the old wagon road from Vincent Gap, and there it is clinging to the mountainside, mill ruins of the Big Horn Mine.

Left: Big Horn Mine 2. The mill appears not so dilapidated back in 1974. Courtesy of Jim Burns

Far left: The entrance to the Big Horn Mine frames the figure of Jim Burns looking out at snowy Mount Baldy in 1974. Courtesy of Jim Burns.

became popular with hikers, inspiring Orchard Camp, a trail resort near a little creek at the halfway point. The buildings are gone now, but Orchard Camp, with its 1,500-year old canyon-oak tree, marked a welcome halfway resting place on last year's trip up and down this route — renovated by volunteers.

George Ellery Hale hiked this same trail in 1903, looking for an observatory site, which led the following year to the establishment of Mount Wilson Observatory. The pioneering work of Hale, Edwin Hubble, and others established this observatory complex as a world leader in solar research and astrophysics, operating full scale today.

Running down Mount Wilson through Idle Canyon, AC100 participants continue along the 1890s railway bed of the Mount Lowe Scenic Railway Complex, which brought visitors up a 1,300-foot incline railway and four-mile trolley ride to resorts that included an observatory.

Next to me, a silver-haired man shielded himself from the wind and gestured to the Los Angeles skyscrapers visible in the haze far below. "On clear days you can see the ocean and Catalina Island," he said. "I've been coming up here for the last 25 years (to Inspiration Point, part of the resort complex.)

Remnants of the once world-famous Mount Lowe Railway operation have resurfaced in the last 12 years — thanks to Brian Marcroft and volunteers.

While hiking on Echo Mountain in 1971, Marcroft discovered some old stone foundation ruins and an enormous bullwheel. Research showed him their role in Thaddeus Lowe's mountain railway tourist attraction, which during four decades of operation lured more than three million visitors, remembered by long-time area residents today.

Top: From the summit of Mount Baden-Powell, the Angeles Crest-100 racers look like toy figures parading across the ridge, on a stage setting with grandiose backdrops.

Above: Scouts make an annual 53-mile Silver Moccasin trek from Chantry Flat to Baden-Powell, where this summit monument commemorates the Boy Scouts founder, Lord Baden-Powell

Below: Gusty winds whip snow aloft on this frigid November day near the appropriately named Windy Gap, about two miles by trail north of Crystal Lake.

Sparkling spray from Cooper Canyon Falls mutes sunlight
patterns on the surrounding cliffs and trees.

Fable asserts
that the notorious

Mexican bandito, Tiburcio Vasquez, hung an old rifle in a tree on a ridge coming out of Cooper Canyon. Over time, the tree grew around the rifle. Ron Huxman, who lived near the canyon some 30 years ago, said that from time to time he'd go search for that tree, but he never found it.

Vasquez hung from a rope in 1875 — which is not legend, but fact.

Above: Lofty incense cedars near Buckhorn Campground guide our way to a secret wilderness garden and an almost hidden waterfall.

Below: Sometimes wildflowers entice us to slow down so that we never reach the intended destination. These wild Canterbury bells, also called California bluebells, Phacelia minor, lassoed us effectively one spring day when hiking above Chantry Flat.

Cyclists pedal along the eight-mile shady service road from along the west fork of the San Gabriel River to Cogswell Dam. The road winds between the river and a woodsy, canyon wall until just before it arrives at the dam, where it seems to veer straight up. A lanky fisherman sauntering along with his pole told me the stream is one of the area's best kept secrets — free of crowds, graffiti, and trash beyond the first mile or so from the highway.

Shh. Be quiet. Astronomers are sleeping!

We only heard a few birds singing and the occasional whir of generators when walking around the Mount Wilson Observatory complex one Saturday morning, for much of the action takes place there at night.

The 100-inch Hooker telescope (the world's largest from 1917 to 1948) partners with several interferometers and solar telescopes to continue astrophysical studies today. The Hubble Space Telescope, named after Mount Wilson astronomer Edwin Hubble, is perhaps the most widely recognized link to this preeminent observatory. Pioneering discoveries made here include: the existence of the sun's magnetic field, recognition that the sun is not at the center of the Milky Way, the existence of galaxies in addition to the Milky Way, and the phenomenon of galaxy recession (which led to the Big Bang theory).

For more information, see Web-sites *www.mtwilson.edu* and *www.mwoa.org*.

"It seemed like a historical gem that was just there and getting worse as time went on," Marcroft said in an interview. Marcroft credits Forest Service volunteer Jim T. Spencer with keeping the story alive until 1992, when together they formed the Scenic Mount Lowe Railway Historical Committee. This group cleared brush to expose foundations, installed signs with historical photos and reconstructed the ramada at Inspiration Point, which is near Easter Rock.

Their work brought a forgotten era to life last year when I wandered about the railway resort foundations on Echo Mountain, tried out an echo-phone placed on its heyday post, walked the 127-curve trolley railroad bed with interpretive photo-signs between Echo Mountain and Ye Alpine Tavern site, and stood at Inspiration Point next to the silver-haired old-timer.

Later I spied him snoozing on a sunny bench a half-mile away at Ye Alpine Tavern site, now a Forest Service trail camp. Perhaps he was dreaming of scenes long ago, for the volunteers have placed historical photos there too.

From the Mount Lowe Railway bed, AC100 runners keep going past Millard Campgroundand head for the finish line in Johnson's Field, Pasadena, before the 33-hour cut-off time.

Thinking back on what was the most inspirational part, Elliott said, "Just finishing the race. It was just an emotional relief that I'd done all this training and then there it was, I was at the end. I had done it."

"I had my met my goal," he added with a big sigh.

In 2003, 71 of the 130 starters finished before the cut-off time, 10 in less than 24 hours. Trail volunteers, crew teams and supporters work as one, making it happen.

Similarly, groups link efforts to protect the mountains' resources, as in the San Gabriel Canyon above Azusa. The Upper San Gabriel Valley Municipal Water District and the U.S. Forest Service to garner volunteers to plant trees in watershed restoration projects. The Forest Service, City of Azusa, the San Gabriel Mountains Regional Conservancy, and others have organized Think River, which gives teachers accredited workshops on local mountain geology, water quality, flora, and fauna.

Sunlight filters through the forest canopy near Chantry Flat, casting an ethereal glow on the yellow and green.

Top: *Interpretative signs along the 127-curve trolley railroad bed show historic photographs of specific locations during the Mount Lowe Scenic Railway's heyday.*

Above: *A massive bullwheel is all that remains of the cable incline that brought visitors to the resort on Echo Mountain.*

Bottom: *Visitors walk softly today about the resort foundations on Echo Mountain, as if spirited away by the Mount Lowe Scenic Railway Resort operation, one of California's most popular destinations during its forty years of operation.*

"I think the whole secret is education, and you have to start when they're little." said Steve Segreto, Forest Service naturalist. Segreto spearheads programs at the San Gabriel Canyon Environmental Education Center, formerly the old Rincon Fire Station. "We're trying to get the community involved," he said, adding that he tells visitors, "This is your forest, and I work for you. You need to take care of your forest."

In April, Segreto repeated these lines to Project Think fifth-graders from Sutherland Elementary School, Glendora, before introducing the day's three projects. Water testing intrigued me, so I traipsed along with one group to a tiny stream, where Barbara Croonquist, Forest Service interpretive specialist, gave the children instructions and supplies to test for ammonia, dissolved oxygen, nitrates, and pH.

"Water is life," Segreto had said, and at a Scouting project four days later I discovered more about the tenuous quality of San Gabriel River water, which accounts for more than 40 percent of the San Gabriel Valley's supply. Also, the San Gabriel River provides critical habitat for the native, 4-inch Santa Ana Sucker, whose count is an indicator of the water quality. These fish had reached the "endangered" status in all three forks, and as of June 2004, Department of Fish and Wildlife decisions about protecting the river water were pending.

Lois Pickens, Forest Service volunteer coordinator, detailed the significance of the sucker's status as she passed out trash pickers to about 23 teenagers and parents gathered around to begin a

Scouting project cleaning trash from the East Fork of the San Gabriel River. Kayla Chang, 15, had organized the April event as part of a conservation elective for the Venturing Award Project with the Boy Scouts of America, USA.

"We take eight tons of trash out of here between Memorial Day and Labor Day each year," Pickens said later while handing out enormous plastic bags. At Baptism Rock, the first clean-up site, the entourage filled their bags energetically with cans, glass, paper and disposable diapers. Kayla's friend, Christie Shu, shook her head at little pools formed by small dams that people had built with rocks. The year before she'd organized a project to break up these dams that change the water's temperature and pH, promoting the growth of bacteria that kill fish.

At the next stop, Cattle Canyon Bridge, the group's mood changed to "yuck." At the water's edge, they stepped cautiously and hoisted trash gingerly with their pickers. Someone commented that rainwater drains the filth into the stream, yet a few teens followed Pickens across the river to retrieve more trash. Near these grim faces, a few children and adults lolled on plastic toys in the water. "This is your drinking water," Pickens called out to the campers under the bridge. One man grabbed a bag sheepishly and picked up some dirty paper plates.

Kayla estimated later that her group brought in 71 bags of trash. "It was a lot more disgusting than anyone expected," she said. The trash situation, however, is reportedly worse all through the summer.

Because our national forests are squeezed with budget constraints, volunteers help fill the gap. The Fisheries Resource Volunteer Corps is one of the groups helping in canyon cleanups. On weekends, these trained, uniformed volunteers monitor the East and West Forks of the San Gabriel River.

"The presence of a uniform makes a huge difference," Pickens said. Besides working with Scouting, school and church projects, she coordinates the San Gabriel River Ranger District's several active volunteer groups, one with llamas. About 100 trained uniformed volunteers patrol, build and repair trails, staff information stations, pick up and pack out trash, haul equipment, and help the Forest Service in sundry ways.

Preserving San Gabriel's treasures is a daunting challenge, like the AC 100. Yet these guardians throughout the range must have heard the words of Dr. Seuss's Lorax:

> "UNLESS *someone like you*
> *cares a whole awful lot,*
> *nothing is.going to get better.*
> *It's not."*

Top: *Project Think fifth-graders from Sutherland Elementary School, Glendora, cross a stream at the San Gabriel Canyon Environmental Education Center, formally the old Rincon Fire Station.*

Middle: *Forest Service interpretive specialist Barbara Croonquist gives children instructions and supplies to test water quality, one of three student projects for the day.*

Bottom: *David Orme picks up trash from the East Fork of the San Gabriel River beneath Cattle Canyon Bridge as part of a river cleanup project. Kayla Chang, 15, organized the work as an elective for the Venturing Award Project with the Boy Scouts of America, USA.*

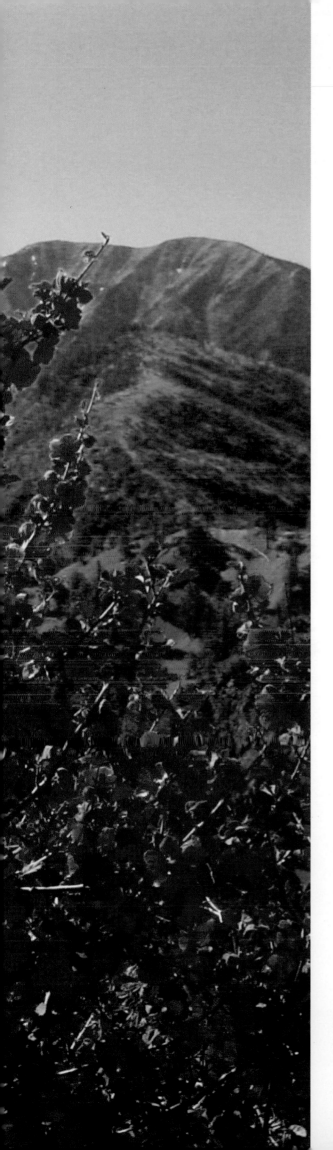

The nation behaves well if it treats the natural resources as assets which it must turn over to the next generation increased; and not impaired in value.

— THEODORE ROOSEVELT
26TH PRESIDENT OF THE UNITED STATES

Album VI

Angel Portraits

Mountain glory comes in many patterns. Fremontia, or flannelbush, Fremontodendron californicum fans out to the heavens before a backdrop of mountains along the old wagon road to Big Horn Mine.

Above: "Hello," I yell through the facsimile echo-phone on Echo Mountain and wait for the faint "hellooo" to reverberate back.

Left: Climbing these steps on Echo Mountain is like stepping back in time, thinking of the millions of visitors who climbed the same steps during the incline railway's four decades of operation — and who looked down on a different San Gabriel Valley.

Mount Baldy beckons in the horizon, seen from the Old Mount Wilson Trail. Built in 1864 by Benjamin Wilson to log timber, the trail through Little Santa Anita Canyon is now a popular hiking route to the top of Mount Wilson.

Previous page: It is not a mirage. You have hiked four and a half miles, waded across the East Fork of the San Gabriel River a dozen times and followed a ridge high above. Then you see it, the ostentatious "Bridge to Nowhere" spanning the river but leading nowhere except to a narrow footpath.

Below: The steep path leads down to the gorge called The Narrows where rushing water tumbles and cascades into churning pools. The disastrous flood of 1938 ended the efforts to link Highway 39 and Highway 2, leaving only the bridge going nowhere.

Upper right: Bush, or sticky, monkeyflowers, Mimulus aurantiacus, seem in their right place, clinging to the cliffs away from the river and near the trailhead.

Lower right: The return trip means a dozen more river crossings, but this time we find better routes around thigh-high holes in the water — and notice this Yucca whipplei, Our Lord's Candle, startling us to find it growing so close to the river.

Above: Check dams look like gigantic Lincoln Log™ structures along the river in Santa Anitia Canyon above Chantry Flat.

Right: Walking down the flower-lined path from Chantry Flat is like entering an enchanted forest, and although Spanish broom, Spartium junceum, is not a native plant, its yellow blossoms brighten the way.

Below: This creamy flower reaches out in simple beauty within a bed of green. A member of the Rock-rose family, the plant near Chantry Flat is not native to California.

It feels like a rain forest along the stream near Chantry Flat, but the tree front and center is a Canyon live oak, *Quercus chrysolepis*.

Opposite: Listen for the music of water when approaching 50-foot Sturtevant Falls, nestled in Big Santa Anita Canyon from Chantry Flat. The falling water sets a mood.

> "Over stone lips
>   the creek leaps out as one
>   divides in spray and streamers,
>   lets it all   go."

A stanza from *"The Flowing"* from Mountains and Rivers Without End *by Gary Snyder.*

Right: The Gabrielino Trail commemorates Native Americans who forged trails in the San Gabriels for hunting game and gathering acorns.

Below: Bush monkeyflowers, Mimulus aurantiacus, brighten many paths along lower mountain reaches, as shown here in the Santa Anita Canyon. The leaves of these winsome blossoms are sticky underneath, hence another common name of sticky monkeyflowers.

GABRIELINO TRAIL

ROBERTS	.7 MI.
STURTEVANT FALLS	2 MI.
SPRUCE GROVE	4 MI.
NEWCOMB PASS	5.1 MI.
DEVORE	9 MI.
WESTFORK	10.4 MI.

Treat the earth well. It was not given to you by your parents. It was loaned to you by your children.

— KENYAN PROVERB

Kim Huxman and her daughter Ali, age four, from Tucson, Arizona, bicycle along the service road to Cogswell Dam, which follows the West Fork of the San Gabriel River. After the ride, Huxman shows Ali ceanothus blossoms, and tells her how as a child at Mount Baldy village school, she (then Kim Rhodes), used to wash her hands in the stream with this so-called "soap plant," alias ceanothus.

Above: California bluebells, Phacelia minor, wave in a gentle breeze, as if cautioning us to take our time winding our way above the San Gabriel Valley to Echo Mountain.

Opposite: The West Fork of the San Gabriel River, like the East Fork, is a popular recreation area, which threatens to jeopardize water quality.

Unexpected panoramas unfold quickly, like this one from a turnout on Highway 2 above La Canada. On this spring evening, we stopped to watch the fading light effects on the peaks and valleys spread out before us.

If we protect what we have and restore what we can, we not only pass on what we have to the next generation, but we pass on something improved, something better to future generations.

— BILL CORCORAN
REGIONAL REPRESENTATIVE, SIERRA CLUB

Tomorrow

Water flows through Cucamonga Creek Canyon, once again free of rusty abandoned cars, junked motorcycles, and beat-up refrigerators because Chuck Medrud, a young Riverside welder, cared enough to keep seeking help.

"I know that canyon like the back of my hand," Medrud said, and when at age 23 he realized that the stream hang-out of his teen years had become a "trash pile" of scrapped cars and rusted appliances, he decided to do something. For about a year, he went from one local, state, and federal agency after another; and he persisted. "I had the will to see it to the end," he said, although sometimes he became discouraged. He solicited help from Bob Watson, owner of Top West End Towing, non-profit groups like the Sierra Club and more than a half-dozen government entities. With their help, Congressman Joe Baca's staff coordinated two community canyon cleanups, the first on December 7, 2002.

Mount Baldy emerges through the trees looking west from the summit of Cucamonga Peak.

Looking down where Cucamonga Creek cuts through
mountains, the canyon appears rugged — and it is.

More than 70 shovel-wielding volunteers dug out 27 stripped, beat-up cars which had been pushed over a cliff and into the canyon and creek. A few weeks later, a helicopter airlifted the excavated vehicles, which Watson's company hauled away. Key to the project's completion, Watson paid for the airlift.

Once aware of the threats, people who love our mountains are responding on many fronts. I believe a caring persistence is rising today, reminiscent of the spirit of John Muir and others who sparked our government's national reserve system, which became our national forests. In 2004, several environmental groups created the Southern California Forests Campaign (SCFC) so that we might enjoy, protect, and restore Southern California's four national forests, Angeles, San Bernardino, Cleveland and Los Padres, restoring their balance and maintaining low-impact recreation that, according to John Monsen, Regional

Once aware of the threats, people who love our mountains are responding on many fronts.

Conservation Organizer SCFC, does not "destroy scenic beauty, scar the land and put wildlife at risk." Monsen adds, "Our every shrinkage pool of open spaces near populated land makes it even more important to protect our magnificent national forest legacy."

In a similar thrust, Californians are responding to words by Pulitzer Prize-winning author Wallace Stegner, "Something will have gone out of us as a people if we ever let the remaining wilderness be destroyed; . . ." Residents are rallying to a call from more than 100 organizations, urging wilderness designation within our state to protect watershed, wildlife, and sustainable recreation opportunities.

Response to these local, regional and statewide appeals confirms what I discovered while writing this book. Countless people, realizing the significance of these mountains in our lives, are working to protect them.

Volunteers carry out parts of cars and appliances on the second community creek cleanup. The work is grueling, but nothing compared to a few weeks earlier when some 70 people dug out 27 cars — stripped vehicles pushed over the cliffs into the canyon stream.

Keller Peak fire-lookout host Paul Labarrere said it best, "I heard the call of the mountains, and I'm doing this." Labarrere volunteers three to four days a month, scanning the forest for smoke and answering visitors' questions.

With our collective awareness of how to make a difference today, our children's children will be able to hear the mountains' call tomorrow.

We need wilderness preserved — as much of it as is still left, and as many kinds — because it was the challenge against which our character as a people was formed. The reminder and the reassurance that it is still there is good for our spiritual health even if we never once in ten years set foot in it. It is good for us when we are young, because of the incomparable sanity it can bring briefly, as vacation and rest, into our insane lives. It is important to us when we are old simply because it is there — important, that is, simply as idea.

— Wallace Stegner, from "The Wilderness Letter, 1960," written to the Wildland Research Center and included in a collection of Stegner's writings, *The Sound of Mountain Water.*

Above: "I heard the call of the mountains, and I'm doing this," says Paul Labarrere, fire-lookout host on Keller Peak. Labarrere volunteers three or four times a month scanning for smoke and answering visitors' questions.

Right: Water flows through Cucamonga Creek Canyon once again free of rusty abandoned cars, junked motorcycles and beat-up refrigerators. It happened with Chuck Medrud's persistence, Bob Watson's towing and airlift support, backed up by non-profit groups working for months with government agencies.

Below: This young man pulls a can from the water, while other people start cleaning up the graffiti at several locations along the creek.

The fragile beauty of these wildflowers is ephemeral, and reminds me of Wallace Stegner's words: "Something will have gone out of us as a people if we ever let the remaining wilderness be destroyed."

Yet these same flowers backed by a cleaner Cucamonga Canyon give me hope that people who clean up canyons and volunteer in myriad ways are making a difference today so that our children's children will be able to hear the mountains' call tomorrow.

Resources

Gagnon, Dennis. *Hike Los Angeles Volume Two*. Santa Cruz: Western Tanager Press, 1992.

McKinney, John. *Day Hiker's Guide to Southern California*. Santa Barbara: Olympus Press, 2001, 1987.

Robinson, John W. *San Bernardino Mountain Trails, 100 Hikes in Southern California*. Berkeley: Wilderness Press, 2003.

Robinson, John W. *Trails of the Angeles, 100 Hikes in the San Gabriels*. Berkeley: Wilderness Press, 2001.

❦ ❦ ❦

Additional References

Bean, Lowell John. *Mukat's People, The Cahuilla Indians of Southern California*. Berkeley and Los Angeles: Univ. of California Press, 1974.

Bean, Lowell John and Lisa Bourgeault. *Indians of North America, The Cahuilla*. New York: Chelsea House, 1989.

Bean, Lowell John and Katherine Siva Saubel. *Temalpakh, Cahuilla Indian Knowledge and Usage of Plants*. Banning, Ca.: Malki Musuem, Inc., 2003.

Bean, Lowell John, Sylvia Brakke Vane, and Jackson Young. *The Cahuilla Landscape, The Santa Rosa and San Jacinto Mountains*. Novato, Ca.: Ballena Press, 1991.

Clucas, Donald L. *Upland Trails, An Early History of Upland and San Antonio Canyon*. Upland, Ca.: California Family House Publishers, 2002.

Fuller, Michael Woodworth. *ISOMATA The Place and Its People*. Idyllwild, Ca.: Idyllwild School of Music and the Arts, 1983.

James, Harry C. *The Cahuilla Indian*. (Copyright 1960, Westernlore Press) Reprinted Banning, Ca.: Malki Museum Press, 1995.

Johnston, Francis J. *The Serrano Indians of Southern California*. Banning, Ca.: Malki Museum Press, 1980.

Krone, Beatrice and Max. Unpublished papers. Idyllwild, Ca.: Krone Library and Museum, Idyllwild Arts, 1949, and The Krone Family.

McCawley, William. *The First Angelinos, The Gabrielino Indians of Los Angeles*. Banning/Novato, Ca.: Malki Museum Press/Ballena Press Coop., 1996.

Robinson, John W. *Mines of the San Bernardinos*. Glendale, Ca.: La Siesta Press, 1977.

———. *Mines of the San Gabriel*. Glendale, Ca.: La Siesta Press, 1973.

———. *San Gorgonio: A Wilderness Preserved*. San Bernardino, Ca.: San Gorgonio Volunteer Association, 1991.

———. *The San Bernardinos, The Mountain Country from Cajon Pass to Oak Glen, Two Centuries of Change*. Arcadia, Ca.: Big Santa Anita Historical Society, 2002.

———. *The San Gabriels, The Mountain Country from Soledad Canyon to Lytle Creek*. Arcadia, Ca.: Big Santa Anita Historical Society, 1991.

Robinson, John W. and Bruce D. Risher. *The San Jacintos, The Mountain Country from Banning to Borrego Valley*. Arcadia, Ca.: Big Santa Anita Historical Society, 1996.

Stegner, Wallace. *The Sound of Mountain Water, The Changing American West*. New York: Penguin Books, 1997.

Woolsey, Ronald C. *Will Thrall and the San Gabriels, A Man to Match the Mountains*. San Diego: Sunbelt Publications, 2004.

SAN GABRIEL MOUNTAINS

Wrightwood

⑫

▲⑪
Mount Baden-Powell

Mount
▲San Antonio
⑩

⑰

⑬

Mount
Lowe ▲

Mount
▲ Wilson

⑮

Cucamonga
▲ Peak
⑭

Burbank

⑯

Pasadena

Pomona

Ontario

Los Angeles

⑨

OUR MOUNTAINS 🍃 *Points of Interest*

SAN JACINTO MOUNTAINS
❶ Idyllwild
❷ Aerial Tramway
❸ Lake Fulmer
❹ Malki Museum

SAN BERNARDINO MOUNTAINS
❺ Lucky Baldwin Mine
❻ Holcomb Valley
❼ Running Springs
❽ Lake Arrowhead
❾ Cajon Pass

SAN GABRIEL MOUNTAINS
❿ Mount Baldy Village
⓫ Big Horn Mine
⓬ Buckhorn Station
⓭ Bridge to Nowhere
⓮ Cucamonga Canyon
⓯ West Fork San Gabriel River
⓰ Chantry Flat
⓱ Switzter Falls